Alien Anthology

Alien Encouters and Area 51

2 Books in 1

Dr. Julia Sanders

Table of Contents

ALIEN ENCOUNTERS

Chilling True Stories of The Paranormal

Dr. Julia Sanders

A series of similar celestial phenomena was reported to have taken place over the skies of Basel, Switzerland in 1566. The Basel pamphlet of 1566, produced by historian Samuel Coccius, described strange sunrises and sunsets while numerous red and black balls fought in the sky. A total eclipse of the moon was also reported. Interestingly while Ufologists regard this as a recorded alien encounter Coccius interpreted it as a religious event.

These types of miracle or sky spectacles were common in the 15th and 16th centuries other notable examples occurred in Wallachia and South Korea.

increased but have also become more detailed.

On the 14th of April 1561 as dawn broke above the ancient city of Nuremberg, Germany its bleary eyed residents witnessed what was later described as an "aerial battle". People reported seeing large black triangular objects in the sky along with spheres, cylinders and various other shapes. Some reports claimed that one of the triangles crashed outside the city walls. A German broadsheet newspaper described the event in detail and illustrated it with a woodcut by engraver Hans Glaser.

Introduction

Since the dawn of time humans have recorded strange objects in the sky. From the scribes of Pharaoh Thutmose III in 1440 B.C.E. who recorded seeing fiery disks in the sky to the ancient Greeks, the general Timoleon claimed that when at sea a fiery torch in the sky had guided his fleet safely home, and the Romans, both Livy and Pliny the Elder record strange lights and shapes in the sky, people have looked up and thought "what on earth is that?"

As time has progressed and literacy has become more common reports of sightings in the sky have not only

As our understanding of the night sky and space has grown; many of these sightings have found explanations in the form of stars, planets or meteor showers. Some however are yet to be satisfactorily explained. Throughout the following chapters we will be looking at some of the best known and most intriguing alien encounters from all over the world.

Aurora and Airships across America

During 1896 and 1897 thousands of people of different ages, classes and races reported seeing "airships" in the skies above America. There is some dispute over when the first sighting was occurred. While a sighting in Sacramento California, on the 19th of November 1896, is largely accepted as being the first some argue that an incident occurred a few days earlier in Winnemucca, Nevada. Either way this heralded an important and busy "airship" era. Between late November and early December 1896 the Sacramento Bee and Union and San

Francisco Call reported numerous sightings of these "airships".

By early 1897 the sightings had spread to Washington. Between February and June of that year Texas had become a hot spot for sightings. All the while public interest in the airships was growing. It was against this backdrop that the Aurora encounter occurred.

1897 was not, until this point, the best year for the residents of Aurora, Texas. A devastating fire and a "spotted fever epidemic" had claimed the lives of many of the town's residents while a boll weevil infestation had laid waste to the local cotton crops, the town's main source of revenue. A further blow had come with the construction of a railroad, which, despite initial hopes that it would serve the town, completely bypassed Aurora. For the 3,000 or so residents of Aurora theirs was very much a dying town.

At around 6 a.m. on the 17th of April the citizens who had not given up and moved away, hoping for better times elsewhere were awoken by the appearance of what was described in the local press reports as an "airship". People watched as the craft appeared to malfunction, stalling in the early morning sky before crashing into a windmill on the property of local judge J. S. Proctor. Debris was reportedly scattered over a wide area.

The airship crash was reported in the Morning News, a local newspaper. The article documented that the crafts pilot was also its sole occupant. It went on to describe that "while his remains were badly disfigured" the rescue party and curious onlookers were able to discern that "he was not an inhabitant of this world".

In 1973 United Press International conducted an interview with Mary Evans. At the time of the incident Mary was 15 years of age and was living with her parents in Aurora. Despite her advancing years Mary clearly remembered her parents telling her that the pilot's body had been buried in the town's cemetery. This was common knowledge amongst the townspeople as was the fact that the remains of the craft were disposed of down a nearby well. This is supported by contemporary accounts such as the April the 19th 1897 edition of the Dallas Morning News, which contained a report by Aurora resident S.E. Haydon describing the pilot as being buried with "full Christian rites" in Aurora Cemetery.

Many years later the former Mayor of Aurora Barbara Brammer conducted her own detailed research into the case and concluded that it was probably a hoax. As we have already seen in the months prior to the crash Aurora had suffered a series of tragic incidents and was in danger of dying out. Brammer's research found that S. E. Haydon was a known practical joker. She came to the conclusion that the crash and subsequent reports of a funeral was Haydon's attempt to keep the town alive.

This theory is supported by the fact that the Dallas Morning News never pursued the story further or allowed S.E. Haydon to write a follow up detailing, for example, the pilots funeral. Further enforcing the idea that the Aurora encounter was a hoax a 1979 article in Time magazine by Etta Pegues claimed that Judge Proctor never had a windmill on his property.

More recent investigations into the case have focused on disproving the claims of sceptics. Recent investigations have shown that there was a structure on the Proctor property, not a windmill but a three-storey water pump. Possibly the two may have been confused over time or it may, at one point, have housed a windmill as well.

As for the craft in the well, today there is no trace. If it was ever there unwitting owners probably removed it in the intervening years. However tests on water in the well have shown that the while the water is normal it does contain large amounts of aluminum.

In 1973 the Mutual UFO Network undertook an exploration of Aurora Cemetery. In the grounds they uncovered many unmarked graves one of which was supposedly marked with a strange UFO shaped marker. The team's metal detector gave off a series of interesting readings from the grave. Permission to exhume the grave was denied.

Later it was reported that the marker had been removed and a three-inch pipe had been placed in the ground. The team's metal detector no longer gave off readings from the grave suggesting that whatever was there had been removed.

Over time many of the cases reported during the 1896/ 1897 airship flap have been explained away as practical jokes, balloons, kites, hysteria or planets and stars mistakenly identified. For many the Aurora encounter sits in this category. For others Aurora is the first properly documented interaction with an alien species and the actions of the townspeople in quickly destroying or burying the evidence has hampered it from being taken as seriously as it deserves.

Whatever the truth of Aurora it is undeniably unusual when considered amongst the wider context of the 1896/ 1897 "airship" flap in that it is one of the few cases which actually involved alien contact. Today Aurora is proud of its alien encounter hosting an annual festival, which helps to keep the town alive.

Roswell

Over the years numerous books, films
and documentaries have been made
attempting to explain the events that
occurred at Roswell, New Mexico.
What follows here is a basic
explanation of the facts followed by an
explanation of how the event became
embedded in the world psyche.

What was later characterized as "the
UFO Wave of 1947" began with 16
alleged sightings that occurred
between May the 17th and July the
12th, 1947, (although some researchers
claim there was as many as 800
sightings during that period).
Interestingly, the "Roswell Incident"

was not considered one of these 1947 events until the 1978-1980 time frame.

Roswell is a city located on the High Plains in southeastern New Mexico. From 1941 to 1967 Roswell was home to the Walker Air Force Base also known as Roswell Army Air Field.

In 1947 W.W. "Mac" Brazel was a 48-year-old rancher working the J.B. Foster ranch, 30 miles south east of Corona, New Mexico. On the 14th of June Brazel, accompanied by his 8 year old son Vernon, was around 8 miles from the ranch house when he came across an area of wreckage about 200 yards wide. The debris appeared to consist of rubber strips, tinfoil, paper and sticks. As Brazel was in a hurry to finish his rounds he didn't pay too much attention to it at the time.

When later asked about the size of the craft Brazel was unable to offer any firm answers as he did not see it fall from the sky and did not see it before it was torn up. He therefore had no idea what size or shape it might have been. When pushed for an estimate Brazel suggested that "it might have been about as large as a table top". The balloon which held it up, if that was how it worked, Brazel estimated as being about 12 feet long. Brazel described the rubber as being smoky grey in color.

After reading in the newspapers about the "UFO wave" Brazel began to wonder if he had found the remains of a craft. Accompanied once again by his son Vernon along with his wife and 14-year-old daughter Betty, Brazel returned to the crash site to gather up the debris. While some accounts suggest that the family returned to the site a day or two later others place it as late as July the 4th.

When it was all collected the tinfoil, paper, tape, and sticks made a bundle about three feet long and 7 or 8 inches thick. The rubber sat in a separate pile, which was 19 inches long and 8 inches thick. Brazel estimated that the entire lot weighed about five pounds.

The family found no sign of metal in the area and also found nothing, which may have served as a propeller although at least one paper fin had been glued onto some of the tinfoil. There were no marks showing ownership or any form of writing on any of the wreckage however some tape decorated with flowers was found. While no strings or wires were found some of the paper had eyelets in it, which suggested that some sort of attachment might have been used.

Brazel had previously found weather balloons on the ranch. He was sure that this wreckage was not a weather balloon.

While Brazel did discuss his find with friends in the nearby town of Corona it wasn't until the following Monday, when he was in Roswell on business, that the authorities were informed. Here Brazel approached sheriff George Wilcox and informed him that he thought he had found a flying disk. Wilcox duly passed on the information to Roswell Army Air Field.

An intelligence officer from the base, Major Jesse A Marcel, and a "man in plain clothes"accompanied Brazel to his home to view the debris. Brazel later reported that despite the men's attempts to reconstruct it they were unable to satisfactorily piece the craft back together. Marcel and the man then took the debris back to Roswell Army Air Field.

Early on Tuesday, July the 8th the Roswell Army Air Field issued a press release reporting that "the intelligence office of the 509th bomb group of the Eighth Air Force, Roswell Army Air Field, was fortunate enough to gain possession of a disk".

Also on the 8th of July a telex message was sent to an FBI official from Fort Worth, Texas. It quoted a Major from the Eighth Air Force, based in Fort Worth at Carswell Air Force Base who described the disk as being "hexagonal in shape" and "suspended from a balloon by a cable". The balloon was estimated to be twenty feet in diameter. The message continued to say that Major Curtan thought the object "resembled a high altitude weather balloon with a radar reflector."

As the explosive press release circulated Colonel W. H. Blanchard, commanding officer of the 509th, contacted General R. M. Ramey of the Eighth Air Force in Fort Worth Texas and ordered that the object be flown to Fort Worth Army Air Field. There Warrant Officer Irving Newton identified the object as a weather balloon with a radar reflector. A second press release, this time from Fort Worth, corrected the original statement confirming the object as a weather balloon.

This seemed to settle the matter and Roswell remained largely forgotten until the 1970s. Between 1978 and 1994 UFO researchers including, Stanton T. Friedman, William Moore and Karl T. Pflock along with the team of Kevin D. Randle and Donald R. Schmitt interviewed several hundred people who claimed to have a connection with the events at Roswell in 1947. These interviews were supplemented with many documents obtained via the Freedom of Information Act and others such as Majestic 12, which was supposedly leaked by insiders. Their conclusion was that at least one spacecraft had crashed near Roswell and the government had covered up the incident as well as the recovery of alien bodies.

This pronouncement sparked the publication of numerous contradictory accounts of Roswell by a variety of authors citing a variety of sources. Numerous locations for the crash were presented as were the number of crafts and aliens involved. This was soon supplemented by numerous movies and documentaries, such as Robert Stack's Unresolved Mysteries, which devoted a large portion of one episode to a "recreation" of the Roswell encounter. All of which fuelled the growing belief that an alien craft had crashed at Roswell and that the U.S. Government had covered it up.

Today the events that occurred on the J.B. Foster ranch in 1947 have been exaggerated to the point of almost mythic levels. The seemingly small pile of debris originally recovered is now believed to be a great amount of debris from an ever-expanding area. Similarly the material recovered has evolved from sticks, paper and tinfoil to exotic materials complete with hieroglyphics.

Currently most Roswell believers agree that there were two crash sites and that at the second site alien bodies (the number of which no one agrees on) were found. The recovered wreckage along with the bodies was taken back to Roswell Army Air Field under tight security. Some cite the seemingly sudden development of technologies such as fiber optics as the U.S. Government exploiting and reverse engineering recovered alien technology.

In response to the growing clamour around Roswell an internal investigation was launched by the United States Air Force. The results were summarized in two reports. The first from 1994 concluded that the material recovered was debris from Project Mogul a military surveillance program using high- altitude balloons.

The second report, from 1997, concluded that reports of bodies being recovered were a mixture of anthropomorphic dummies used in various military projects and a combination of people misremembering events, hearsay and hoaxes. Those who believe that alien bodies were recovered from Roswell claim that this is disinformation.

Despite the vast amounts of research and claims of credibility that have arisen surrounding Roswell the fact is much of this evidence is based on verbal accounts. Although there is no firm evidence that a UFO crashed at Roswell, many still believe that what occurred on the ranch outside Corona was a government conspiracy. B. D. Gildenberg has called the Roswell incident "the world's most famous, most exhaustively investigated, and most thoroughly debunked UFO claim". This hasn't stopped Roswell becoming a Mecca for UFO hunters.

Kenneth Arnold

A second notable incident that occurred during the 1947 "UFO wave" was the Kenneth Arnold encounter.

Kenneth Arnold was born on the 29th of March 1915 in Sebeka Minnesota. He spent much of his childhood in Scobey, Montana before attending the University of Iowa. At the time of his encounter Arnold had been employed by the Great Western Fire Control Supply in Boise, Idaho for seven years. This job took Arnold all around the Pacific Northwest and he often flew between destinations.

A skilled and experienced pilot Arnold had clocked over 9,000 flying hours almost half of which were devoted to Search and Rescue Mercy Flyer causes. In short Arnold was a respected businessman and experienced aviator; he bore all the hallmarks of a reliable witness.

On the 24th of June 1947 Arnold was flying a CallAir A-2 from Chehalis, Washington to Yakima, Washington. Arnold had made a brief detour from his original route after learning of a $5,000 reward for the discovery of a U.S. Marine Corps C-46 transport plane, which had crashed near Mount Rainier.

The skies were completely clear and there was a light wind. Just after 3:00 p.m. at about 9,200 feet near Mineral, Washington Arnold gave up his search and started to head east for Yakima. It was then that he saw a bright flashing light, similar to sunlight reflecting in a mirror. Arnold, worried another aircraft was close to him, scanned the skies but could only see a DC-4 around 15 miles away.

Around 30 seconds after that first flash of light Arnold saw a series of bright flashes in the distance to his left, north of Mount Rainier, around 20 to 25 miles away. Realizing that these were not just reflections in his aeroplane's windows Arnold began to watch the objects. He would later describe them as flying in a long chain like a flock of geese.

Thinking they may be a new type of jet Arnold studied them for a tail or other telltale signs. He could find none. The objects, nine in total, seemed dark in profile against the snow covered backdrop of Mount Rainier. Occasionally they gave off a bright light.

At times Arnold said that they seemed so thin and flat that they were practically invisible. Their movement was akin to a saucer skimming across the water. He estimated their angular size as slightly smaller than the distant

DC-4, possibly about the width between the outer engines- around 60 feet.

Arnold would later revise this estimate, realizing that the objects would have to be quite large for him to see any details at that distance. After comparing notes with a United Airlines crew that had experienced a similar sighting 10 days later, he placed the absolute size as larger than a DC-4 airliner (or greater than 100 feet in length). Army Air Force analysts would later estimate 140 to 280 feet.

Arnold watched as the crafts, which stretched out over a distance of around 5 miles, moved on a more or less level horizontal plane weaving from side to side "like the tail of a Chinese kite". He estimated that they reached speeds of around 1200 miles an hour- much faster than the P-80 jets of the time. The encounter left Arnold with an eerie feeling but he suspected it was probably a test flight of a new aircraft.

Landing in Yakima at about 4:00 p.m. Arnold told Al Baxter the airport general manager of his encounter and soon the entire airport staff had heard the story. As Arnold continued on to an air show in Pendleton, Oregon he was unaware that someone at the airport in Yakima had telephoned on head to tell them his story.

On landing Arnold found that his story preceded him. He spent a while discussing his encounter in detail with pilot friends. Some suggested that he had seen some form of guided missile. Despite earlier thinking of similar solutions Arnold was not entirely satisfied with any of these possible explanations.

The next day, June the 25th, reporters interviewed Arnold at the offices of the East Oregonian in Pendleton. They found Arnold to be a reliable witness and his detailed story left many convinced that he was telling the truth. Interestingly it was from these interviews that the term "flying saucer" originated.

As Arnold's story spread around America the man himself quickly grew tired of his newfound fame. He complained that a preacher had told him the crafts were harbingers of doom and that one lady had run screaming from a cafe when he entered. Despite his distaste for celebrity the interviews kept on coming and on the 7th of July two stories were printed in which Arnold suggested that the crafts were of extraterrestrial in origin.

One of the many consistencies in Arnold's story is that throughout all his interviews he always insisted that if the craft weren't of military origin then they were extraterrestrial.

Aside from being a credible witness with a consistent story another factor in the Kenneth Arnold encounter being one of the most credible ever recorded is the amount of supporting testimony from numerous, unconnected individuals. A prospector named Fred Johnson was on Mount Adams at the time of Arnold's flight and reported seeing similar crafts to Arnold. L. G. Bernier of Richland, Washington wrote to the Oregon Journal on July 4th claiming to have seen strange objects over Richland heading towards Mount Rainier. Also in Richland, Ethel Wheelhouse reported seeing flying disks at about the same time as Arnold's sighting.

An investigation by military intelligence in early July found yet another witness- a member of the Washington State forest service who had been on fire watch at a tower in Diamond Gap, 20 miles south of Yakima. This person saw "flashes" at 3:00 pm on the 24th over Mount Rainier. Similarly Sidney B. Gallagher in Washington State also reported seeing shiny disks flashing in the sky. Altogether there were at least 16

reports of UFOs in the Washington
State area on that day. However the
pilot of the DC-4 that Arnold reported
as being in his vicinity at the time saw
nothing unusual.

The military investigation conducted
by Lt Frank Brown and Capt. William
Davidson of Hamilton Field,
California interviewed Arnold on July
1st. They concluded that Arnold was a
credible witness and was not making
up his encounter. Formally, however,
the Army Air Force insisted that
Arnold had seen a mirage.

Later, a second secret investigation by
Army Air Force Intelligence with the
FBI looked at some of the best UFO

sightings, the Kenneth Arnold encounter included. They concluded that the sightings were not imaginary or adequately explained by any known natural phenomena.

Sceptics have argued that what Arnold and the others saw was either a mirage or meteors. Some have even suggested the objects were Pelicans. Ufologists and supporters of Arnold have refuted all these theories.

During a 1950 interview with journalist Edward R. Murrow, Arnold claimed to have seen similar objects on three other occasions and suggested that other pilots in the northwestern region of the U.S. had seen similar things. Until his death in 1984 Arnold maintained that if the objects he had seen were not made by the science of the American military then they must have been of extraterrestrial origin.

The McMinnville Photographs

On the evening of May the 11th 1950, having just fed the rabbits Evelyn Trent was making her way back to the family farmhouse just outside Sheridan, Oregon. As she neared the farmhouse Evelyn happened to glance up at the sky. Despite the day drawing to a close it was still fairly light. Light enough for Evelyn to clearly see a strange metallic disk-shaped object hovering in the sky

As the craft made its way silently across the northeastern sky Evelyn watched its progress. Realizing that she had never seen anything like this before Evelyn called for her husband to come out of the farmhouse to look at the disk. Like his wife Paul Trent was also unable to identify it.

Later the Trents would estimate that the object was around 30 feet in diameter and around quarter of a mile away from where they were standing. It did not spin; instead it appeared to glide, creating a breeze as it moved through the air. The craft was completely silent and neither could see any sign of life.

Despite being mesmerized by the strange object Paul eventually remembered that he had a camera inside the farmhouse. Hurrying to retrieve it he briefly left Evelyn alone to watch the craft. Quickly Paul returned with his Roamer camera and was able to take a photograph.

As Paul fumbled with the camera's cumbersome controls the craft tipped slightly before slowly accelerating to the west. As it did so Paul managed to take a second photograph. From inside the farmhouse Paul Trent's father claimed to have also briefly seen the object before it flew away. The Trents estimated that the encounter lasted for about half an hour in total.

In the days before digital photography the Trents didn't see Paul's photographs immediately. Almost a month had passed by the time the film was finally developed. While they waited the Trents didn't discuss their sighting with anyone outside the family for fear of being ridiculed or not taken seriously. When the film was developed the couple was relieved to see that the two photographs showed exactly what they had seen that evening- a strange craft floating through the sky.

Emboldened by the photographic evidence Paul casually mentioned the incident to his banker Frank Wortmann. Wortmann was intrigued enough to display the photographs in his bank's window in McMinnville. As a result of Wortmann's actions the photographs soon came to the attention of the local newspaper the Telephone-Register. (Today the paper operates under the name News-Register.)

The editor of the newspaper dispatched reporter Bill Powell to the Trent farm to interview the couple. Powell interviewed Paul and Evelyn separately but heard the same story from them both. He also borrowed the negatives to the pictures. Subsequently on June the 8th the Telephone-Register ran both photographs on its front page alongside a headline proclaiming "At Long Last- Authentic Photographs of Flying Saucer [?]".

As public interest in the photographs grew the story was picked up by International News Service (INS) and circulated to other newspapers around America. On the 26th of June 1950 Life magazine published cropped versions of the photographs alongside a photograph of Paul Trent and his camera.

It was around this time that the negatives to the photographs were lost. While Life magazine had promised the Trents that they would be returned they informed the Trents that the negatives had been misplaced. In 1967 the negatives were found in the files of the United Press International (UPI) news service- UPI and INS had merged in the intervening years.

Instead of being returned to the Trents the negatives were then loaned to Dr William K. Hartmann. Hartmann was an astronomer who, at the time, was employed as an investigator for the Condon Committee- a government funded UFO research project based at the University of Colorado Boulder. Around the same time Hartmann interviewed the Trent family and concluded that they were sincere and didn't seem to be making up their story. Indeed the Trents had never received any money from the photographs and Hartmann could find no evidence that this was a publicity stunt concocted by the couple.

In Hartmann's analysis he concluded that "This is one of the few UFO reports in which all factors investigated geometric, psychological, and physical, appear to be consistent with the assertion that an extraordinary flying object, silvery, metallic, disk-shaped, tens of meters in diameter, and evidently artificial, flew within sight of two witnesses."

It was only after Hartmann had finished his investigation and returned the negatives to the UPI did they inform the Trents that the negatives had been rediscovered. In 1970 the

Trents asked Philip Bladine, then editor of the News- Register, for the return of the negatives. While Bladine received the negatives back from the UPI he never passed them onto the Trents. In 1975 Bruce Maccabee an optical physicist for the US Navy and Ufologist discovered the negatives in the files of the News- Register, after conducting his own study of the negatives Maccabee finally returned them to the Trents.

During the 1980s Philip J. Klass and Robert Sheaffer, journalists and sceptics, conducted their own research into the case and concluded that it was a hoax. They argued that that the shadows in the photographs were inconsistent for the time of day they were taken. Klass and Sheaffer theorized that the object was likely a model hanging from power lines visible at the top of the photographs. This led to Hartmann withdrawing his positive assessment of the case.

Despite the work of Klass and Sheaffer, Maccabee remains firm in his assessment that the photographs show a "real physical" object in the sky. He argued that the cloud conditions at the time accounted for the inconsistent shadows. Maccabee believed that the analysis he had done on the negatives showed that the "sighting lines did not cross under the wires" and as Klass and Sheaffer did not account for this he was unconvinced by their argument.

The McMinnville photographs are among the best publicized in UFO history. While sceptics and believers continue to argue over the images authenticity both Paul and Evelyn Trent went to their graves insisting that the encounter was genuine. Today McMinnville is home to America's second largest UFO festival after Roswell.

Kelly-Hopkinsville Encounter

Kelly is little more than a smattering of houses a couple of miles north of Hopkinsville in Christian County, Kentucky. The surrounding area is green and flat with ploughed fields dominating the landscape broken intermittently by clusters of green trees.

Up until the events of the 21st of August 1955 the Sutton family of Kelly, would have been described as a "typical Kentucky family."

Glennie Lankford (50) was the widowed matriarch of the family. It was she who rented the farmhouse that the family lived in. Glennie's two sons from her first marriage, Elmer "Lucky" Sutton (25) and John Charley "J.C." Sutton (21), as well as their respective wives, Vera (29) and Alene (21), and Alene's brother O.P. Baker were with her in the house that night as were Glennie's children from her second marriage: Lonnie (12), Charlton (10) and Mary (7). In addition to the Sutton tribe Billy Ray Taylor (21) and his wife June Taylor (18) were on hand to witness events. The Taylors like Lucky and Vera Sutton were itinerant carnival workers.

At about seven o'clock that evening as Billy Ray Taylor had gone to draw water from the well when he saw a bright light streaking across the evening sky, disappearing beyond a tree line somewhere in the distance. Taylor excitedly returned to the farmhouse to tell the others what he had seen. Unsurprisingly Taylor's claims to have seen a UFO were not taken seriously by the Suttons, who thought a shooting star or meteor a far more likely explanation.

As the families settled down for the night Taylor's story seemed forgotten. Around an hour later the frantic barking of the family dog rudely disturbed them. Hearing other strange noises from outside and assuming that there were intruders on the property

Lucky grabbed his shotgun. Accompanied by Billy Ray, Lucky Sutton went outside to investigate.

As they scanned the tree line for signs of intruders Lucky and Billy Ray saw something moving. They watched dumbstruck as the first of the creatures emerged from the trees. Lucky took aim but as quickly as he could shoot at it another would appear elsewhere. The creatures seemed impervious to the bullets from Lucky Sutton's shotgun. When one did appear to have been hit it would float to the ground before disappearing.

Lucky and Billy Ray retreated back inside the farmhouse. Along with

Lucky's brother J.C. and O.P. Baker they claimed to have gone through box after box of ammunition as they vainly tried to quell the unrelenting tide of creatures. Meanwhile the women encouraged the children to hide under their beds before taking shelter themselves.

The terrifying onslaught continued for the next three hours. At times a face would appear at the window only to be greeted with a hail of bullets. On other occasions the creatures appeared to be on the roof looking for a way inside. Once, when the men were brave enough to venture outside, Taylor felt his hair being grabbed by a huge claw like hand.

Eventually, worried that the men may kill each other, Glennie Lankford managed to calm the situation. With everyone able to think more clearly the families decided that the best option was to make a run for it.

The officer on duty at Hopkinsville Police Station had probably been expecting a quiet night, after all nothing much ever happens in rural Kentucky. It was a warm summers night as the clock struggled lazily to the hour- eleven o'clock. The silence of the night was suddenly shattered by the sound of cars being driven at speed. The screeching of tires outside the police station suggested that the officer's night was about to be disturbed.

A group of eleven desperately worried people hurried into the police station. They were all highly agitated and clearly afraid. To the surprise of the bewildered officer the group desperately begged for help claiming to have been "fighting them for nearly four hours".

The officer did his best to calm the group down before they told him their story. Lucky Sutton and Billy Ray Taylor claimed to have been shooting at "twelve to fifteen" short dark figures that had repeatedly "popped up in the doorway or peered in through the windows". While the police were reluctant to believe that aliens had landed they were concerned that the local citizens had been engaged in a shootout. Four city police, five state troopers, three deputy sheriffs and four military police from the nearby US Army Fort Campbell were all dispatched to the Sutton's farmhouse.

Upon inspecting the property they found substantial evidence of gunfire- spent cartridges along with numerous holes in windows and door frames however they found no trace of the little creatures that had supposedly plagued the family. They also found no trace of the UFO landing that Billy Ray Taylor had claimed to see.

With the family calmed and reassured the law enforcement and army left the premises suggesting they should go to bed. When the officers returned the next day they found no sign of the families. Neighbors told them that they had "packed up and left" for Evansville, Indiana after the creatures had returned around 3:30 in the morning. Long before the Suttons reached Indiana their story was becoming a part of local folklore.

Unsurprisingly the attack on the Sutton property received widespread coverage in both the local and national press. Throughout the coverage the description of the creatures seems to vary. They ranged in size from two feet to four feet while they are only described as "little green men" in later accounts. Details such as pointed ears, claw like hands and yellow glowing eyes seem to vary from depending on which report you read.

The inconsistencies in the story and lack of physical evidence have led many to question the veracity of the Kelly-Hopkinsville encounter. Some have speculated that the aliens were in fact Great Horned Owls and that a form of hysteria led to the Suttons and Taylors getting carried away. A meteor shower that was reported at the time could account for Billy Ray Taylors UFO.

Defenders of the Kelly Hopkinsville case claim that the creatures were possibly gremlins or goblins and argue that the number of witnesses involved and the extended length of time over which the encounter occurred point to it being something more than territorial owls. Either way the official investigations never recorded a hoax, simply marking the case as unexplained.

Despite the many doubts the Kelly-Hopkinsville encounter has become firmly lodged in popular culture. The town of Kelly holds an event entitled the Kelly "Little Green Men" Days on the third weekend every August. While numerous books and films have been inspired by the case- the 1986 film Critters is one such example.

Whatever really occurred that night be it a meteor and a pair of territorial owls or little green men from outer space the legend of the Kelly Hopkinsville encounter continues to grow.

Antonio Vilas Boas

The 1950's saw a spate of UFO sightings all over the world. One of the most interesting cases of this so-called "UFO Flap" is that of Antonio Vilas Boas.

On the family farm in Sao Francisco it was not unusual for 23-year-old Antonio Vilas Boas to work through the night such was the heat of the day. The night of October the 16th 1957 was one such night. From his vantage point in one of the fields Boas could clearly see a bright red star in the night sky.

Boas stopped his work to watch the light. This wasn't the first unusual light to have been seen at the farm. For the previous two weeks both Boas and his brother had noticed a bright light in the sky.

Boas watched motionless, as the "star" seemed to grow larger. After a moment he realized it was heading straight for him. Too afraid to move Boas watched as the light grew in size revealing an egg shaped craft with a red light at its front and a rotating cupola on top. Three spidery legs extended from the craft as it landed in the field.

At this point Boas decided to flee. As he attempted to do so the engine on his tractor died. When Boas attempted to escape on foot a five-foot humanoid in grey coveralls and a helmet seized him. Boas later described its eyes as being small and blue while it spoke in a series of barks or yelps. Three similar humanoids appeared from the craft and aided the first in subduing the farmer before taking him inside.

Once inside the craft Boas was better able to observe his captors. They all wore a "tight-fitting siren-suit" which appeared to have been made of an unevenly striped, grey material. These suits reached all the way up their necks. There they seemed to be joined to a helmet that was made of a grey material "that looked stiffer and was strengthened back at nose level." The helmets obscured everything except the humanoids eyes, which were protected by glasses.

Boas thought that the height of the humanoids helmets suggested that their heads were either twice the size of a normal, human head or that there was something else hidden beneath them. From the helmets came three silvery tubes, Boas was unsure what these tubes were made of. One tube was located in the middle of the helmet; the other two tubes were on either side of the helmet. From there the tubes ran into the humanoids suits: the center tube into a spot where the backbone is while the two side tubes slotted in "under the shoulders at about four inches from the armpits". Boas was unsure how these tubes were attached and could not work out their purpose.

The room Boas found himself in was small and square. There were no furnishings and it was brightly lit, Boas compared it to "broad daylight". The light came from recessed square lights in the smooth metallic walls. An opening appeared in, what had appeared to Boas, a seamless wall and the humanoids led Boas through it into another room.

Unlike the first this room was furnished. An oddly shaped table stood at one side of the room and was surrounded by several chairs. All were made from the same white metal.

The humanoids grabbed Boas before starting to undress him. Despite Boas' protests he was powerless to stop them. Once naked Boas was rubbed all over with a "thick, clear odorless liquid" before being taken to a third room.

As Boas entered this room he noticed the door had a series of red hieroglyphic like inscriptions on it. Two of the humanoids proceeded to take a blood sample from Boas' chin. This left a series of small scars; when Boas was later examined Doctors recorded these marks.

Boas was left sitting on a featureless "foam rubber like" grey bed in the middle of this room for about half an hour. During this period Boas described how a gas was pumped into the room from holes above his head. This gas, while quick to dissolve, left Boas feeling nauseated as if he was being suffocated. After being sick in a corner of the room Boas found his breathing eased.

A while later a naked woman entered the room. She had long, peroxide blonde hair and big blue eyes. She didn't wear makeup and had very high cheekbones, which gave the impression of a pointed face. Her lips were thin to the point of being invisible.

Boas noted that she was thin and short, possibly only reaching up to his shoulder. Her skin was white but her arms were freckled. While her hair was blonde her pubic and underarm hair was bright red.

Boas claimed that they would spend an hour together engaging in various sexual acts before the woman finally pulled away. Curiously during this encounter the woman declined to kiss Boas, preferring instead to nip his chin. When the deed was done they were joined by one of the original humanoids who took the woman away. Before leaving Boas described her as rubbing her belly before pointing up to the sky. Boas took this to mean that she was now pregnant and intended to raise their child in space.

Boas' clothes were returned to him before he was taken back through the craft. Feeling calmer Boas was now more able to take notice of his surroundings. He described the walls as being smooth and metallic, there appeared to be no windows.

Whilst in what appeared to be the control room Boas noticed a box with a glass top that had the appearance of a clock. It had one hand and marks that would correspond to the placing of numbers on a clock. Boas attempted to take the clock as a memento of his encounter but was prevented from doing so by one of the humanoids.

Boas was taken on a tour of the craft, which he was later able to describe in great detail. The tour complete one of the humanoids led him to a ladder, which descended into the field below the craft. As soon as he was clear of the craft Boas turned and watched as it rose up, its tripod legs retracting, before disappearing into the sky.

By the time Boas returned to his tractor it was around 5:30 in the morning. He estimated that he had spent over four hours in the company of the humanoids.

In the weeks after his encounter Boas suffered from nausea and weakness as well as developing headaches and lesions on the skin. It was during this period that he contacted a journalist by the name of Jose Martins who was known to be interested in UFOs. Upon hearing Boas story Martins contacted Dr Olavo Fontes from the National School of Medicine of Brazil. Fontes like Martins had an interest in UFO cases.

Fontes examined the farmer and concluded Boas was suffering from mild radiation sickness after being exposed to large doses of radiation. That Boas was able to recall his encounter in detail, without the need for any form of hypnotic regression, impressed both Fontes and Martins.

Interestingly while the Boas encounter first came to light in February 1958 it didn't gain much traction in the press until the early 1960s.

When the attention did come Boas quickly became disheartened, feeling that his was a credible story undeserving of all the criticism and skepticism it received. Some sceptics claimed that Boas had invented his encounter, borrowing details from other reported cases to make his own story more believable. Boas soon withdrew from public life to complete his studies and qualify as a lawyer. Throughout his life Antonio Villas Boas stuck to the story of his alien encounter.

Mindalore

Our next story takes place in the closed society of apartheid era South Africa. The mining city of Krugersdorp can be found in the West Rand; around 45 minutes' drive from Johannesburg. It was here, in the suburb of Mindalore that the Quezet family lived.

On the night of January the 3rd 1979 Mrs. Meagan Quezet was sitting in her lounge trying to finish the book she had been reading. As the clock approached midnight her twelve-year-old son Andre entered the room unable to sleep. While Andre made them both a cup of tea Meagan became aware that the family dog, Cheeky, was barking outside. Realizing that Cheeky was loose in the street, and afraid that he would be hit by a car, Meagan called Andre to help her catch the dog.

The Quezet property was located roughly in the middle of Saul Jacobs Street. Meagan and Andre walked along the street towards its junction with Tindall Road. Beyond Tindall Road, around 12 meters further up, is a second road, Chamdor Road. This had been built as a connecting link between the factories in Chamdor and the Lupaardivel Industrial area and was not connected to the lower Tindall Road. Chamdor Road was mainly used by heavy, industrial traffic during the day, at night very little traffic used the route.

When they reached Tindall Road, Meagan and Andre saw Cheeky along with most of the neighbourhood dogs barking frantically at a bright pink light on the higher Chamdor Road. Meagan thought that a light aircraft had come down on the road- the light seemed to be too high above the road to be a police car or any other sort of vehicle. As a nurse Meagan felt duty bound to see if she could help. With this in mind the pair continued up to the top road, making their way over a patch of uneven, overgrown grass before clambering up an embankment.

The nearer that Meagan and Andre got the more obvious it became that the light didn't belong to a plane. Despite being cloaked in a very bright pink light the craft appeared to be a metallic lead color. While the pink light seemed to be cloak the craft Meagan could see source from which the light may have come. From an opening they could see inside the craft. The same pink glow seemed to emanate from within.

Meagan would later describe the craft as being "egg-shaped from the top down", which appeared to have been cut straight across its bottom. At the bottom of the craft four thin, "spider like" legs supported it. A sucker pad at the bottom of each leg fixed it onto the road. Meagan estimated it as being around 12 feet high and 16 feet wide.

From their vantage point from the top of the embankment Meagan and Andre had a side on view of the object. Feeling more confused than afraid they quietly speculated that it could be some kind of experimental craft. As they continued to slowly approach the craft 5 or 6 men stepped out of the opening onto the ground. While one or two of the men, Andre and Meagan were never entirely sure which, disappeared from their view around the far side of the craft two of the men remained near its center, almost as if they were guarding it. The final two men came to the side nearest to Meagan and Andre.

The men were wearing identical suits, which covered them from head to toe, making it impossible for Meagan or Andre to discern any muscles or other defining features. Later Meagan would say that she thought that the suits were white but Andre saw them as pink. With the exception of two of the men, one on the far side and the one nearest to Meagan and Andre, their heads were also covered. The man nearest Meagan and Andre had thick, dark curly hair and a beard.

Meagan, standing on a slightly raised embankment, had the impression of looking down on them. Meagan was 5 foot 5 and the men came up to her chin. They were slender in build. Andre noted that one of the men on the far side bent down to pick up some sand from the ground on the side of the road before letting it trickle back down through his fingers.

Meagan and Andre described the two men nearest them as having a conversation. While one spoke in a high-pitched voice using singsong sounding words the other appeared monosyllabic in his answers. They could not hear actual words just the sound of the conversation. Meagan thought it sounded Chinese but found it too high pitched to accurately discern.

After a moment the man doing all the talking seemed to notice that Meagan and Andre were watching them. He said something to his companion. The bearded man turned to look at Meagan. His skin was olive, Middle Eastern in color. He bowed low, to the waist, and said something that Meagan took to be a greeting.

Throughout this exchange his eyes never left Meagan's. Despite this, and being quite sure that they were normal, Meagan had the impression that they were translucent as though she could look through them. Meagan felt herself drawn to him. She said hello before nervously laughing.

For the first time Meagan began to get the feeling that something was not right. She told Andre, who was now standing slightly behind his mother, to run home and get his father. Frightened, Andre didn't need to be asked twice.

As Meagan continued to stare at the men they conversed in monosyllables. Before she knew any time had passed they had returned to their craft. Meagan didn't remember seeing them board or the door closing.

Meagan became aware of a buzzing noise akin to a swarm of bees in a hive. The legs of the craft elongated to about three times their length raising the craft to an overall height of around 20 feet. Andre who had been making his way down the embankment stopped when he heard the buzzing sound. Meagan stepped back afraid of what was going to happen next.

The legs of the craft telescoped inside it as it hovered for a few seconds before shooting off into the night sky. The clouds were very low that night and Meagan could see the pink light shooting up into the clouds. While the craft disappeared in around 30 seconds the clouds seemed stained the same shade of pink for a while after.

Meagan was joined once again by Andre and they both stood there staring at the clouds, shocked. While they estimated that the episode lasted for around ten minutes it seemed much longer. Upon returning home Meagan decided not to wake her husband up as there was nothing he could do about it.

The next day no traces were found on the road.

Today while other similar encounters are far better known the Mindalore encounter is comparatively forgotten.

The Broad Haven Triangle

Following a spate of sightings across the world in 1976 Welsh Ufologist Randall Jones Pugh predicted that a spate of events would follow in Wales in the very near future. While not many people took Jones' prediction seriously even those who did found what happened next to be extraordinary.

Pembrokeshire in the south west of Wales is one of the most picturesque parts of the U.K. Much of its coastline, including the town of Broad Haven, forms the Pembrokeshire Coast National Park. It was against this prettiest of backdrops that the West Wales flap of 1977 occurred.

As they played in the playground of Broad Haven Primary School during lunchtime on the 4th of February 1977 a group of 15 schoolchildren claimed to see a silver cigar shaped UFO in the fields behind the school. Some of the children, aged between 9 and 11, also saw a silver man with pointed ears emerge from the craft. While the teachers and dinner ladies dismissed the story as fantasy, children are often prone to exaggeration and flights of fancy, so adamant were the children that after school had finished for the day they reported their sighting to the local police station.

The headmaster of the school, Ralph Llewellyn, had initially dismissed the pupil's claims, when they saw the craft some children had ran into the school to fetch the headmaster. Mr. Llewellyn annoyed that they were disturbing his lunch break, told them that he "couldn't be bothered to look" and sent the children back outside to play. Later, after learning of the visit to the police station, Llewellyn became intrigued by the children's persistence and asked them all to draw what they had seen. He was amazed at how similar their pictures were.

Just under two weeks later on the 17th of February teachers and dinner ladies at the school claimed to have seen the same craft in the field. One of the dinner ladies believed that she had seen a creature boarding the craft.

Encouraged by Randall Jones Pugh the story soon made its way into the national media. Journalists flocked to this remote part of the Welsh coast from all over Britain. UFOs and aliens quickly became the hot topic of discussion in Wales and by spring people were interpreting stars and planets in the sky as flying saucers and little green men. Some were even seeing silver humanoids wandering the countryside at night.

Sitting in an isolated position overlooking the dramatic Stack Rocks,

Ripperstone Farm was, at this time, home to dairyman Billy Coombs, his wife Pauline and their young children. It was here that much of the activity of the Broad Haven Triangle seemed to occur.

Over the space of a year the family experienced repeated encounters with strange crafts and unexplained lights. Often these encounters seemed to interfere with the family's electricity supply sending items haywire and electric bills spiraling. Pauline Coombs seemed to be the focus of the attention and claimed to be experiencing encounters on a monthly basis. Once the car she was driving was chased by a fiery, oval shaped object along the narrow county lanes.

Even more extraordinarily the couple claimed that one on occasion a herd of cows was teleported from a locked and secure field into an adjacent farmyard.

The most famous incident at Ripperstone farm was the appearance of a 7ft tall figure in a spacesuit whose blank face stared eerily through the living room windows. By the time the local police force had arrived there was no sign of the spaceman. The policeman who attended the farm later described them, as "the most frightened family I have ever been to see."

While much of the activity centered on Ripperstone Farm numerous sightings were reported all over the county. For example on the 13th of March a young boy named Steve Taylor claimed to have seen an orange, glowing disk in the sky. As he watched it a black dog ran past him.

Taylor followed the dog into a nearby field where he saw a large domed object. Next to it stood a tall man with high cheekbones, "like an old man", who was dressed in a one-piece suit. The man began to approach Taylor.

Frightened the teenager lashed out. Curiously his first punch hit nothing but air. Taylor fled. When he eventually got home the family dog growled at him as if he were a stranger.

At the same time, in nearby Milford Haven (around 8 miles from Broad Haven) a 17-year-old girl claimed to have seen a 3 ft. humanoid standing on her bedroom windowsill watching her.

Also in Milford Haven, on April the 7th Cyril John (64) had risen at 5:00 am to undertake a trip from his home to London. It was then that he saw a light shining into his bedroom window. On closer inspection John described it as an egg-shaped object, silver grey in color with an orangey- red light on the top of it.

The craft was around 4ft in diameter and seemed to rock gently in the air. Near it was a 7 or 8 ft. tall humanoid that John said was floating in mid-air like a "free-fall parachutist". The figure was dressed in a silver-grey suit with no visible facial features. Mr. John claimed that both the craft and spaceman seemingly hovered in the air motionless for around half an hour before moving slowly away.

Less than five minutes' drive from Broad Haven is the quaint village of

Little Haven. Here the owner of Haven Fort Hotel, Mrs. Rosa Glanville, reported that she was woken at 2:30 am on the 19th of April by a strange noise and lights outside. Looking out of her bedroom window Mrs. Glanville saw an object which she described as an "upside-down saucer" around the size "of a minibus" sitting in the field next to the hotel. 2 "faceless humanoids" with pointed heads were also in the field. Mrs. Glanville felt a heat so intense that she thought it was burning her face. The heat seemed to be coming from the multicolored flames, which were emanating from the craft.

As landlady of a famously haunted hotel Mrs. Glanville was not easily scared. She called out to the humanoids demanding to know what they were doing. Getting no response Mrs. Glanville went to rouse other residents of the hotel hoping that they could bear witness to the strange occurrence. When she returned to the window a few minutes later the field was empty.

With the encounter over Mrs. Glanville returned to bed. The next morning, remembering the events of the night before, Mrs. Glanville went to check the area where the craft had landed. There she found flattened grass and scorch-marks. Interestingly the landing site overlooked a field, which contained a Royal Observer Corps bunker.

Concerned Mrs. Glanville contacted her M.P., Nicholas Edwards, who in turn alerted the nearby RAF Brawdy air base. People from the base subsequently visited Mrs. Glanville and assured her that RAF Brawdy were not responsible for the events she had witnessed. They also urged her not to publicize the case as it might alarm the public. Sadly in the small community of Little Haven this was impossible, the story spread like wildfire.

Squadron Leader Tim Webb, who oversaw pilot training at Brawdy, confirmed that the "spacemen" people were describing did not match anything worn by base personnel. Interestingly Webb's son Michael was one of the children who say the UFO at Broad Haven Primary School. Webb told The Observer that he believed his son "implicitly" saying, "I've yet to see a UFO but I think there has to be something supernatural or paranormal."

It was during this period that the suggestion the spaceman was a worker from one of the local oil refineries wearing their protective suit was first put forward.

Back at Ripperstone Farm one incident stands above all the rest and the amount of witnesses to it mean it can't be easily dismissed. In June 1977 Mrs. Coombs returned from taking the children to a Silver Jubilee party to find her husband distressed and upset. He said that he had looked out of the window and noticed a strange silver car approaching the farmhouse.

In the car were two men in black suits. One got out of the car and approached the house. Feeling uneasy Billy had decided not to answer the door, instead pretending that nobody was home. The visit of the men to home of the Coombs family was witnessed by their next-door neighbor Caroline Klass, a nurse.

As Klass was putting rubbish in the outside bin one of the men appeared next to her. She described him as having strange, waxy skin with a high forehead, slicked back black hair and cold, unblinking eyes. In a thick foreign accent he asked where Mrs. Coombs was. Caroline Klass told him that she didn't know and quickly returned to her home.

Later that day Klass was talking to her friend Rosa Glanville of the Haven Fort Hotel. Mrs. Glanville told Klass that her daughter Anna, a student, had been alone in the hotel when a silver car had pulled up outside. The two men in black suits had entered the hotel and had asked for Mrs. Glanville by name. Anna sent them away but noticed that as they left their car made no noise on the gravel.

Despite RAF Brawdy claiming that the incidents had nothing to do with them and the MOD claiming to have "no record of unusual activity in the area" it seems that a discreet investigation was launched. Papers released a couple of years ago show that on the 14th of June 1977 the head of S4 (Air) (the MOD branch responsible for UFO sightings) asked the RAF Police to make discreet enquiries about the events in Wales.

Sadly no report on what the RAF investigation uncovered remains, if it has it will probably never be, released. However a secret briefing on UFO policy from December 1977 the head of S4 was quoted as saying that from time to time the public interest in UFOs increases, "there was some concern in Wales, although the RAF Police thought this could have been the work of a practical joker."

Indeed in 1996 Glyn Edwards a local businessman and member of the Milford Haven Round Table confessed that he had been responsible for the sightings of the 7ft spaceman. A silver lined asbestos suit borrowed from the local oil refinery with a solid in-built helmet was his costume. He and another member of the Round Table had come up with the idea after hearing of the encounter at Broad Haven Primary School.

Evans recalled that he had "visited the garden of a certain lady, who later called the police that I had to dive into a hedge because she appeared to be aiming a rifle or a shotgun at me."

While this accounts for at least some of the spaceman sightings other events are still unexplained. In 2015 Dave Davies, one of the schoolchildren who saw the original sighting, was interviewed by the Mirror newspaper. He said that despite the cynicism of others and the bullying that he had suffered he stood by what he saw that day. Many of his classmates feel the same way.

Local journalist Hugh Turnbull had reported the story for the Western Telegraph, the areas local newspaper. He believed that something military was behind the encounters. Others favored a more extreme solution, suggesting that aliens had an underground base beneath Stack Rocks in St Brides Bay. The claimed that UFOs were often seen to hover above the rocks before disappearing, supposedly diving under the water.

Another popular explanation was that despite official denials the range of military bases in the area was responsible. North of Broad Haven was a rocket testing station at Aberporth while Brawdy trained Hawker Hunter pilots and housed both a Tactical Weapons Unit and a US Navy underwater research station (later revealed to be a unit responsible for tracking the movements to Soviet submarines).

Interestingly when RAF Brawdy closed a few years ago, sceptics may have assumed that the UFOs would also leave the area. However this hasn't been the case. To this day cigar-shaped UFOs are seen in the area.

Despite attempts by journalist Ray Gosling to debunk the sightings in the area many witnesses still stick doggedly to their stories. It seems that the truth of the Broad Haven Triangle is yet to be revealed.

Kelly Cahill

The Kelly Cahill encounter is possibly Australia's most well-known Alien encounter.

The Cahill family was an ordinary Australian family living in the Melbourne suburb of Belgrave. As the clock approached midnight on August the 8th 1993 the Cahills- Kelly, her husband and their three children, were driving home through the Dandenong foothills after visiting friends. It was then that they noticed the lights of a rounded craft in the sky above them.

The craft seemed to hover silently above the road. The family observed that different colored lights were discernible on the bottom of the object. Kelly Cahill later stated that it was so close to the ground she thought she could see people looking out of its windows. Suddenly the craft zoomed away, disappearing as quickly as it had appeared.

The family continued their journey home keeping one eye on the sky in case they should see it again. It was then that they were practically blinded by an intense bright light. Frightened by the light Kelly's husband kept driving, desperate to get his family to safety.

As they sped away Kelly found herself feeling very relaxed as if the disappearance of the light was reassuring. She thought she might have blacked out but when asking her husband if she had he didn't respond.

Upon their arrival home Kelly could smell a foul odor, like vomit and began to sense that something was missing. What was missing was an hour of their journey.

Later, as Kelly undressed for bed, she noticed a strange triangular mark on her naval.

That night Kelly dreamt that she was back at the site of the encounter. As she sits at the side of the road she sees her husband being led out of the craft by a creature that Kelly assumes is female. She tackles the creature before blacking out.

Kelly then finds herself on the far right of the field away from the UFO. Next to her is a body, which seems to take on a human form. A middle-aged woman is repeatedly screaming "Murderess" at her. Kelly finds herself overcome with grief, unaware that she has killed anybody.

A hand is placed on Kelly's shoulder. She is led into the craft and soon finds herself in a small room. In it, next to a table, stood one of the creatures. The creature tells her she hasn't killed anyone, it explains that they were using her sense of morality to overcome her fear. For some reason Kelly thinks that she knows this creature.

Also in the room is a Bible belonging to Kelly, it had disappeared from the family home a few weeks previously. The creature then gives Kelly a choice: she can come with them but must leave the Bible behind. The dream ends with the creature giving Kelly the bible.

A few days after the encounter Kelly's husband found the missing Bible in the family car.

For the next few weeks Kelly suffered from what she described as a general malaise and was hospitalized twice, once for severe stomach pain and the second time for a uterine infection. It was during this period that she began to remember further details from the night.

Kelly recalled a large UFO, around 150 feet in diameter, hovering above a gully. She also remembered that the first time they saw it her husband had stopped the car and they had both walked towards it. Kelly remembered feeling calm but afraid. She felt as though they were being drawn to the craft. She also remembered that on the opposite side of the road another car had stopped to look at it.

As the Cahills approached the craft they saw a creature Kelly described as black, "not a black color but black as if all matter was removed". She thought it was soulless. It was around seven feet tall with large red eyes, which glowed in the night.

After a moment Kelly noticed that there were "heaps" of these creatures all in the open field beneath their craft. They appeared to be in small groups, one of which glided towards Kelly and her husband covering the distance effortlessly in only a matter of seconds.

In the distance a second group of creatures approached the other car.

Kelly recalled feeling that the creatures were evil and that she had clung to her husband for protection, fighting the urge to black out. Kelly's next memory was of being back in the family car.

Further dreams led to Kelly recalling much of what happened that night.

In many of the dreams she sensed a presence, which warns her to be calm, however Kelly felt it had a sinister motive. Later on she would experience her legs being lifted and drawn out of the bed. Again the presence was present. In the dreams

Kelly eventually sees the creature leaning over her, about to kiss her naval.

Conversely Kelly's husband recalls hardly anything of that night. While he remembers the UFO he does not recall stopping the car or the alien creatures.

With her husband unable to remember and unwilling to discuss events Kelly felt increasingly isolated. As she struggled to make sense of the encounter Kelly contacted various universities and aviation authorities. Despite her extensive attempts Kelly was unable to find any satisfactory answers to what she experienced that night.

Unlike many other encounters the Cahill experience is not without corroboration. As well as the car that Kelly had seen a third car was parked further up the road with its lights off. According to the occupants of car two, Bill, Jane and Glenda, the third car contained one visible occupant- a man who was gazing fixedly toward the UFO.

Both Jane and Glenda were able to recall being on the craft. Like Kelly they described the creatures as being tall and black. Unlike Kelly they did not describe them as having red eyes.

The women did not think that they were abducted instead feeling as if they exercised free will throughout.

Curiously while the women didn't remember seeing each other while on board the craft each was aware of what was happening to her companion.

Much of what Kelly experienced also occurred to both Jane and Glenda. Unlike Kelly neither Jane nor Glenda suffered any after affects.

Like Kelly's husband, Bill seems to have had only a limited role in the encounter. While he was able, with the help of hypnosis, to recall smells, sounds and the sense of activity Bill does not have any visual memories of the encounter.

That Jane, Glenda and Bill experienced a strikingly similar encounter to the Cahills adds credence to the case. This is further enhanced by the fact that neither group knew each other and was unable to discuss their encounter with each other before being interviewed.

Ufologists later visited the site of the encounter and found a possible related ground trace and low-level magnetic anomaly at the encounter site.

Today some consider Kelly Cahills encounter to be an elaborate hoax. While parts may have been exaggerated or invented in the constant retelling the story is yet to be disapproved. Kelly Cahill was considered to be a reliable, honest person by those who knew her and had no reason to invent the story.

AREA 51

The Truth Behind Roswell and the
Area 51 Conspiracy

Phil Coleman

Introduction

Just when did this place "happen"? When did people start to notice there was something there that was not there before?

Actually, August 1, 1955, when there was a high-speed test with the first U-2.

Area 51 has always been full of mystery and conspiracy theories.

It is a huge area of wasteland that was called for years simply: Area 51. To make it sound a little better, there was a period that it was called "Paradise Ranch," but who do they think they were fooling?

For years, it was not even allowed to be placed on a map of any kind.

There have been tons of theories and mystery shrouded in Area 51. There have been deathbed confessions regarding Area 51 that at one time were on YouTube but now they have been removed.

So, what do you say when a road to get there is named "Extraterrestrial Highway?"

The Whistleblowers of Area 51

Bob Lazar – he claimed that in 1989 he worked in Area 51, in the underground near the Papoose Lake inside the Papoose Range. He stated he had been contracted to work along-side alien spacecraft that the U.S. government had there in Area 51.

Bob was a physicist that worked in Area 51, so he was no dummy, and he had been sent there to work on reverse engineering of the aircraft's that had belonged to the aliens that had been captured and brought to the underground vault.

Bob had pictures of this little alien. If it is true, it makes one feel immensely sorry for this lifeform.

One thing that seems to stand clear among those who believe Lazar's stories. Much of the current technology we use is a result of reverse engineering from alien space craft; includes all kinds of technology like radios all the way to superconductors.

It is said that there is no way, that the human race as it is now could have possibly developed these technologies this fast without some alien model.

Many people disregard what Bob says as fiction are offended at the fact of what he claims, including a guy named Merlin, who has spent years and years speaking with Area 51 former employees who are angered about the fuss over E.T.

They say, "This is Earth technology, just good ole American ingenuity. Not any extraterrestrial stuff."

A 71-year-old mechanical engineer, Bill Uhouse, claimed he had been a former employee for Area 51 during the 50's. He claims that he worked on a "flying disc simulator" that had been on that crashed UFO and was being used to train U.S. Pilots. He also said that he worked with an alien named "J-Rod" and described him as a "telepathic translator."

Bill said J-Rod was Grey in color. Bill said that he worked with J-Rod so they could build a flight simulator to train the Air Force pilots to fly advanced USAF stealth air craft.

J-Rod himself had been the pilot of the UFO that had crashed.

Uhouse said that to talk to J-Rod, he used Grey alien technology that had been adapted to be used for humans. He was able to communicate with the Grey alien via telepathy that was assisted by very sophisticated translator software.

J-Rod taught humans how to fly the UFO.

Uhouse went on to say that there were different races within the Greys of the aliens.

They included Tall Greys, Short Greys, and then Greys with a size comparable to humans.

Uhouse died in 2009. It can no doubt be deduced going by deathbed confessions that extraterrestrial races and their civilizations are out there and they are technologically and scientifically far more advanced than we are.

It is the belief that during the administrations of Harry Truman and Dwight Eisenhower, is when construction began on the alien-government facilities. They were built for homes for the Grey, Reptilian, and Tall White Alien scientists.

SUPPOSEDLY, Eisenhower signed treaties with the extraterrestrial races.

The agreement signed with the Greys, Reptilians included that our government would let them perform bio-genetic research to design advanced forms of alien-human hybrids.

Our U.S. government allowed the aliens to get their hands on a limited number of humans to use as guinea pigs, for their bio-genetic research.

Conspiracy folks say Grey and Reptilian aliens needed to do this to save their races from extinction.

In return, the aliens give the U.S. access to alien technology, in particular, aerospace.

Now, there are rumors that Aliens are breaching their agreement and capturing more humans than they should. That sounds a little hard to believe - Almost conspiracy theories.

U.S. authorities cannot stop the violations. The facilities underground is armed with vast laboratories and special workshops. The underground areas have segments where the extraterrestrials live and captured humans are used as research guinea pigs are held as prisoners.

According to Ulhouse, to stick to their part of the bargain, there could be as many as hundreds or even thousands of the Grey aliens that are working with the PENTAGON!

Boyd Bushman, an ex-aerospace engineer also sent to Area 51 for a very long time has pictures of humanoid beings that do not belong to anything of this world. He confirms that staffs working in area 51 are a mixed lot of extraterrestrial beings and earthlings.

In 2004, there was a guy by the name of Dan Burisch (pseudonym of Dan Crain) said he worked on alien virus cloning at Area 51 beside an alien named "J-Rod." Burisch's credentials are much in question; however, as he was working as a parole officer in Las

Vegas in 1989 while he was also supposed to be earning a Ph.D. at New York State.

Existence of Area 51

They say that it is a facility of the U.S. Air Force and it is a remote part of Edwards Air Force Base that is highly classified. It is found in the Nevada Training and Test Range.

According to the CIA (Central Intelligence Agency, there are several names for this area, some of which are KXTA, Groom Lake, Homey Airport, Dreamland, Home Base, Paradise Ranch, and Watertown.

There is airspace around the field that is a Restricted Area 4808 North.

The main purpose for this base to the public is unknown; but based on past evidence; it supports developing and testing of weapons systems and experimental aircraft.

The intense secrecy that shrouds this place has caused it to be a frequent subject of UFO folklore and conspiracy theories.

The base itself has never been declared secret, but everything going on there is Top Secret and Sensitive.

July 2013 when the Freedom of Information Act requested information in 2005, the CIA for the first time acknowledged the bases existence.

Area 51 is in Nevada in the southern portion of the western U.S. and 83 miles northwest of Las Vegas. Smack in the middle and on the south shore of Groom Lake sits a large airfield of the military.

The U.S. Air Force acquired this land in 1955; they said to use for flight testing of aircraft, namely at the time the Lockheed U-2.

There was, in the beginning, a six by 10 mile base of sorts which is now called the "Groom Box." But now it measures 23 x 25 miles and is restricted airspace.

This area shares a border where the location of 739 and 928 nuclear tests were conducted by the United States Energy. The Yucca Mountain has a nuclear waste dump site 44 miles away from Groom Lake.

Groom Lake being a salt flat is used primarily, or so they say for runways for the Nellis Bombing Range Test Site airport.

The size of the lake is about 3.7 miles by 3 miles. This Lake is 25 miles south of the town Rachel, Nevada.

Where the name Area 51 came from is still unclear. The best guess is it comes from a grid numbering system by the Atomic Energy Commission. Area 51 is not part of the system, but it lies next to Area 15. No one knows.

In 1864 lead and silver were found in the south part of Groom Range. In the 1870's, Groome Lead Mines financed the mines giving it the name. Mining continued until

1918 and resumed after WWII until the early 1950's.

When WWII came along, the airstrip on Groom Lake started beginning service. They called it Indian Springs Air Force Auxiliary Field. It had two dirt runways that were 5000 feet long.

The test facility at Groom Lake for the U-2 program was established in 1955 by the CIA (Central Intelligence Agency) for developing the Lockheed U-2 Strategic Aircraft.

The director at the time, Richard Bissell, Jr., was told that due to the extreme secrecy of the project, the pilot training programs and the flight testing would not be done at Edwards Air Base or Palmdale.

An inspection team went out to Groom Lake. When they flew over it, they supposedly knew within thirty seconds that it was the perfect place.

The lakebed was a perfect landing strip for which they could do their testing of aircraft, and the mountain ranges would protect them from prying eyes. The CIA had the AEC acquire the land and designate it "Area 51" on the map.

Johnson himself called it "Paradise Ranch" so that the workers would be more encouraged to move to somewhere in the middle of nowhere. Most of the men just called it "the Ranch." Some of them called themselves Ranch hands.

Initially, it had a few shelters, some workshops, and trailer homes. At the end of three months, it had one paved runway, a control tower, three hangers, and essential accommodations for testing staff.

The only amenities were a volleyball court and a movie theater. There was a mess hall, fuel storage tanks, and several water wells.

July 1955, CIA, Lockheed staff, and Air Force started arriving. July 24th, they received its first U-2 delivery on a cargo plane.

Lockheed technicians came on a Douglas DC-3. To keep things secret, staff flew into Nevada on Monday mornings and went back to California Friday evenings.

In August 1959, Project OXCART was established. It was for antiradar studies, engineering designs, aerodynamic, structural tests and later on work on the Lockheed A-12.

October 1960 saw the beginning of a four-year construction project for Area 51. It was a double shift that worked.

The CIA received eight USAF F-101 Voodoos, two T-33 Shooting Star trainers, one C-130 Hercules for transporting cargo, U-3A for administrative use, a helicopter to be used for search and rescue, Cessna 180 to be used for liaison use, and an F-104 Starfighter to use as a chase plane.

February 26, 1962, the first A-12 test aircraft was trucked in from Burbank, reassembled and made its first flight April 26th. By then there was 1,000 staff members.

At first, anyone not connected with the testing be done at the time would be taken into the mess hall. They quickly stopped this because it was disrupting work and was just impractical.

The Area also saw the first Lockheed D-21 drone test on December 22, 1964. In January 1967, it was decided to phase out the CIA A-12 program.

After losing Gary Powers' U-2 over the Soviet Union, there began several discussions about using the A-12 OXCART like a drone. The Air Force finally agreed in October 1962 to the study of a high altitude, high speed, and drone aircraft. It would be called D-21.

The first launch of D-21 was on March 5, 1966, and it was successful. It flew 120 miles due to a limited amount of fuel.

The second flight was successful in April 1966, and the drone flew 1,200 miles, reaching 90,000 feet and Mach 3.3.

July 30, 1966, D-21 trial suffered from a non-start of the drone itself after separation and caused it to collide with the launch aircraft. The two crewmembers ejected and landed 150 miles off shore in the ocean. One was picked up by a helicopter; the other survived the breakup and the ejection, but drowned when water from the ocean filled his pressure suit.

Kelly Johnson said that was enough and canceled the entire program. There had been several D-21s already made, and instead of dumping all of them, Johnson proposed to the Air Force that they might launch them from a B-52H bomber.

Later than summer of 1967, modifying the D-21 (now called the D-21B) and the B-52Hs were done. They could restart the testing program. Test missions took off from Groom Lake and launches were over the Pacific.

The first test was on September 28, 1967, and it ended up in complete failure. There were several more flights, including two over China, one in 1969 and one in 1970. July 1971, Kelly Johnson got a wire that said cancel the whole D-21B program. The drones that were left went to dead storage.

In 1993, the D-21B's were released to museums.

During the Cold War, the United States tested and evaluated Soviet fighter aircraft that had been captured. Area 51 was supposed to have been where they were taken. As a matter of fact, they were supposed to have quite a collection of Soviet aircraft.

In August 1966, an Iraqi fighter pilot defected and flew his MiG-21 on to Israel. He had been ordered to drop napalm on Iraqi Kurd villages. His aircraft was brought to Groom Lake within a month's timeframe.

In 1968, they gained two MiG-17s that were transferred from Israel because two Syrian air force lieutenants got lost.

In early 1982, they were testing YF-117A airplanes.

There are other aspects of activities of Area 51 that involved tests of 'acquired' Soviet-radar systems gotten covertly. In November of 1970, there was a project that was called HAVE GLIB. Once account of this project was that they used 'actual Soviet replicas

and systems set up as a complex' around
Slater Lake.

The USAF gave these places name such as
Kay, Mary, Kathy and Susan and arranged
everything so it would be just like a Soviet
air defense complex.

Now, when they declassified the F-117
program, the Air Force decided to bring in
two other air programs into Area 51.
Neither of these projects ever led to a
production of an operational fleet however.
Both have been declassified. There are some
pictures and some fact sheets giving some
details about the two secret programs which
never really got off the ground.

There was one plane that was developed by the Northrop group along with the USAF and DARPA. It was TACIT BLUE, a battlefield plane to be used for surveillance and it was also known as the "Whale."

They started working on it in 1978 and got to finally fly it at Area 51 February 1982. The program for this air craft stopped in 1985 and it had flown a total of 135 times.

The fact sheet on this project showed that the goal was to 'demonstrate that with curved surfaces would make a difference in low radar return signal' and that TACIT BLUE could go to the front line of the battlefield without any fear of being seen on the enemy radar.

Then there was another plane that Area 51 worked on with McDonald Douglas (bought out in 1996 by Boeing) called the "Phantom Works" and some called it the Bird of Prey," after all it did resemble the Klingon from Star Trek.

But, it was declassified in 2002 because its techniques basically were already becoming obsolete.

Interestingly, there were two other projects that were connected to Area 51. One of them was used in a raid on May 2, 2001 and it was the raid that took down and killed Osama Ben Laden.

It was the stealth helicopter that took our Navy Seals up to the Abbottabad compound where Ben Laden was hiding. The other piece was a RQ-170 stealth drone that had been used to monitor what was going on in and around the compound.

The RQ-170 is an unmanned drone and it is intended to be used to provide surveillance and reconnaissance for our soldiers. This drone alone can save numerous lives and get in and out and send back invaluable information to our men.

Safety of our soldiers should be the first thing that is thought about for them, their families and for our country.

Commuters to Area 51 get there by travel on an unmarked Boeing 737 or 727. The planes leave from McCarran Airport in Las Vegas.

EG&G, the defense contractor, owns this terminal. Each plane uses the same name, "Janet" followed by three digits for calling into the control tower.

Airspace above Area 51 is called R-4808 and is totally restricted to any and all commercial and military flights not coming from the base itself.

Area 51 is classified as a (MOA) Military Operating Area. The borders have no fence, but orange poles mark the perimeter and warning signs are posted. The signs warn that photography isn't allowed and trespassing will result in a fine.

There are other signs that are more sobering: "Security is authorized to use deadly force on people who insist on trespassing."

Of course, the conspiracy folks wonder how many have died because they got caught tromping around on the grounds of Area 51. Most believe, however, that the trespassers are not dealt with so harshly.

Men in pairs that do not appear military are patrolling the perimeter. The guards are probably civilians hired from contract companies.

Most people call them "camo dudes," just because they wear desert storm camo. Camo dudes usually are seen driving around in a four-wheel-drive vehicle of some sort.

It seems that camo dudes have instructions to avoid the intruders and only act as deterrents. If someone appears to be an intruder, camo dudes will put a call into the sheriff, and he will deal with them.

There have been times when camo dudes have confronted trespassers, taking their film or any recording devices and trying to scare the trespassers. Sometimes, a helicopter will fly over or hover around to harass or scare.

With all the sensors planted everywhere around the base, no one can get past them. They are supposed to detect movement, but there are those who think they can tell the difference between human and animal.

Since Area 51 is a wildlife area, it would seem to be important that a warning device could not be tripped by animals.

Some feel that they are ammonia sensors being able to tell between human ammonia and animal ammonia.

One Rachel resident, Chuck Clark got his hand on several sensors from around the perimeter. He was found out and ordered to put them back or face some serious fines. Reportedly, he complied.

Everyone is interested in what is going on in Area 51 today. Here are a few ideas, not saying they are in stone, but very real possibilities:

- A transport aircraft to move troops out and in areas of conflict without ever being detected. Many saw this as a critical need.

- Stealth helicopter. Some say that these already exist and are in use, but have never been revealed to the public.

- There is a need for a stealth airplane so it can neutralize ground targets.

- Other research projects that are rumored are proton beams, anti-gravity devices, and cloaking technology.

The A-12 plane is a very impressive handsome aircraft that was developed in

Area 51. It flies at speeds higher than 2,200 mph and must have 186 miles to turn around.

Many people still do not believe that man landed on the moon or ever set foot there and that it was staged out in Area 51. They also say that the astronauts tested life support systems and lunar rovers at the atomic testing grounds just next door.

Legal Status of Area 51

October 22, 2015, a judge signed papers taking land that had belonged to a Nevada family since the 1870s and turned it over to the USAF so they could expand Area 51.

This family had owned the property since Abraham Lincoln was president.

The Sheahan Family had owned the old mine and knew they had a terrible battle going up against the U.S. government. They knew ahead of time that it would probably be taken from them through eminent domain.

The government condemned the property one month after the family declined their offer of a $5.2 million buyout. They knew their land was worth a lot more than that because of all the mineral rights for it and the number of acres it contained.

The land has a lot of ore in it and on the land, there is mining equipment, buildings and the remains of loved ones buried who worked the mines since 1870.

The family has also had to suffer from radiation drifting from nuclear shots during the 1950s and the 1960s.

The family feels like it has been a 60-year Black Ops, AEC, CIA and you could go on forever said Joe Sheahan, the heir.

Since the air force has condemned the property, the value of the land is now only $1.5 million.

The judge said that the land that was being taken was to address safety and security connected with testing and training.

How wrong can this be?

The government's amount of information that they are willing to tell is at best very little. The area around the Lake is off-limits permanently to all civilians and even to regular air traffic of the military. Security checks are constant; no weapons or cameras of any kind are allowed.

1994 saw litigation from five unnamed contractors that were civilians and the widows of two contractors, Robert Frost and Walter Kasza against the USAF and the US EPA (Environmental Protection Agency).

They were represented by Jonathan Turley, a law professor at George Washington University. Their allegations were that they had been exposed to large amounts of unknown chemicals that were burned in trenches and open pits at Area 51.

Biopsies taken from these individuals were analyzed, and in the biopsies, there were found high levels of dibenzofuran, trichloroethylene, and dioxin. They also alleged that they had suffered skin, respiratory and liver injuries due to their working at Area 51; and that this fact had caused the mortality of Frost and Kasza.

The suit asked for compensation for their injuries, due to the claim that the USAF had not handled the toxic materials properly, and that the EPA had failed to enforce the Resource Conservation and Recovery Act (the act that governs the handling of dangerous materials).

The families also wanted detailed reports about the chemicals to which they had been exposed, in hopes that those still living might be better served medically.

Congressman Lee Hamilton, a former chair of the House Intelligence Committee, told Lesley Stahl on 60 minutes, "The USAF is classifying all this information to protect Area 51 from a lawsuit."

And the government wonders why the public does not trust them?

The President still raises the issue every year trying to determine the Groom exception. This, raised by the President and other very specific wording used in other communications by the government, is the only real recognition the U.S. Government has given that Groom Lake is more than a part of the Nellis complex.

There was an unclassified memo that went out on safe handling of Nighthawk F-117 material that got posted on an Air Force web site apparently inadvertently in 2005.

This material was what had been discussed by the complainants in the lawsuit. The information the government had declared was classified. The memo was gone quickly after journalists were made aware of it.

In 2007 in December, it was noticed by pilots that the base was now appearing on their navigation systems latest Jeppesen revision. The airport code being KXTA and was listed as "Homey Airport."

This inadvertently published information of airport data was soon followed by an announcement that student pilots needed to be warned about KXTA, and they were not to ever consider it a destination or waypoint.

There is signage all around the base perimeter that advises deadly force will be used against all trespassers.

Early most mornings, some eagle-eyed visitors can spot lights in the sky moving around and up and down. It is not a UFO. In reality, it is the semi-secret commuter airline contracted that they call "Janet" that transports employees in from Las Vegas to Area 51.

Fiction or fact, the alien theme is a huge tourism draw. In 1996, Nevada renamed Route 375, "Extraterrestrial Highway" and gave destinations like the Alien Research Center and an Alien Cathouse which is supposedly the only alien-themed brothel in the entire world.

If you are planning on walking to Area 51, plan carefully. It is a desert. Bring snacks, bring the right clothing for the cold nights and the horrible hot days and bring LOTS of water.

Your phone will probably not work nor you're GPS. Have real maps. It will be hard to find gas stations, so have spare tires and extra fuel.

Whatever you do, DO NOT trespass. Arrests and heavy fines await you for this infraction.

UFO & Other Conspiracy Theories

Along with its secretive reputation and the connection to aircraft research, along with odd reports of unusual phenomena, has caused Area 51 to focus on modern UFO and the conspiracy theories surrounding them.

June 24, 1947, Kenneth Arnold reported that while he was piloting his private plane, he saw something that was flying in the sky like a saucer would if you skipped it across the water. Thus, the name of the "flying saucer" was born.

Some of the activities causing all of this include:

- The examination, reverse engineering, and storage of crashed spacecraft with aliens (including items that were supposed to be recovered from the UFO crash site at Roswell), the study of occupants (dead and living), aircraft manufacture based on technology used by aliens.

- Joint undertakings or meetings with extraterrestrials.

- Developing of exotic weapons of energy for Strategic Defense Initiative or other programs for weapons.

- Developing means to control the weather

- Developing time travel and technology for teleportation.

- Developing of exotic and unusual propulsion systems that are related to the Aurora Program.

- Activities aligned with one world government (Illuminati) or Majestic 12 organization.

Many theories involve concern the underground areas at Groom or Papoose Lake. They claim transcontinental railroad underground system and alien based engineering technology.

During the mid-1950's, civilian aircraft would fly under 20,000 feet while

Military would fly under 40,000 feet. When the U-2 started flying, it went above 60,000 feet, and one of the side effects it caused was an increased sighting of UFOs.

They were usually seen during the early evening. When pilots were flying west and saw U-2's silver wings reflecting the setting sun, it would give the aircraft its own "fiery" appearance.

Many of the UFO sightings came to USAF Project Blue Book, which is where UFO sightings were investigated, by air-traffic controllers and by letters sent to the government.

Most of the UFO sightings could be dismissed, but they could not reveal to the people who wrote the letters the actual truth about what they did see.

Veterans working in Area 51 will admit that their work while there in that time frame more than likely prompted many of the UFO sightings.

The shape of OXCART had a wide, disk-like fuselage so it could carry large amounts of fuel. Commercial pilots flying over Nevada at around dusk could look up and see the bottom of an OXCART flying overhead at 2,000 plus miles per hour and with the suns reflection it would make anyone think UFO.

They felt the rumors helped keep Area 51 in secrecy. And, so it did.

In June 2015, the head of NASA did confirm that aliens did in fact exist, but they were not hidden at Area 51.

We know today, which thousands, if not millions of other planets, many probably very much similar to our 'earth' exist. So, it seems fair to say that we will find out that life or evidence of life elsewhere will be found.

People living in towns nearby report sightings of strange lights that appear as if are hovering over Area 51. Per eye witnesses, the lights do not look like lights on fighter jets or any other earthly aviation type units.

Supposedly there is an autopsy video (**http://proofofalien.com/the-truth-of-roswell-alien-autopsy-video/**) of the alien that was taped during the autopsy held inside Area 51. This is said to be evidence that Area 51 has a strong connection with the little guys.

The corpse of this particular alien is thought to have been from the Roswell site in New Mexico.

When you go this website, you will find that this documentary was found to be a hoax, as real as it looked. Ray Santillilli, declared that he received $100,000 and got his film from an 82-year-old American who was a retired photographer.

You will notice that this video is no longer available for viewing, but the corpse on the website sure looks real if you are into looking at dead aliens.

July 1947, the time of the alleged Roswell, New Mexico alien crash was what really put Area 51 on the map.

It was the first week of July 1947, and a UFO crashed on the ranch of W.W. "Mack" Brazel in Roswell, New Mexico.

Later, Brazel found some debris from close to the crash site, so he and wife, Loretta and Floyd Proctor's son got on their horses and rode out to check on their sheep since there had been a bad thunderstorm the evening before.

As they were riding out to where the sheep were, Brazel noticed odd pieces of what looked like some metal scattered here and there over a pretty large area.

When he looked closer, he noticed something that looked like a shallow trench that was several hundred feet in length and it had been gouged down into the ground.

Brazel said what was so odd was the metal. He had never seen any metal like that before. They gathered some of it up and took the large pieces to his shed and a piece or two over to show the Proctors.

Mrs. Proctor remembers when he came to the house with the strange looking metal.

The Proctors told him it might be something from one of the UFOs everyone had been seeing and he needs to tell the Chaves County Sheriff, George Wilcox.

So, a couple of days later, Brazel went into Roswell and reported the weird incident to the Sheriff. He, in turn, reported it to Major Marcel who served as an intelligence officer and was stationed at Roswell Army Air Field.

History of UFO crashes was kept in a book that UFO researchers, Kevin Randle and Don Schmitt say that they kept their research recorded in and it did show that military radar was tracking some flying object they could not identify over southern New Mexico for about four days. They noticed on July 4th, 1947, that the object had looked like it went down about 30-40 miles from Roswell.

The book records that eyewitness Bill Woody, who lived near Roswell to the east, said he remembered being outside that night when he saw a brilliant light plunge to the earth.

Well, the debris site was then closed to everyone for several days so the wreckage could be cleaned up. Randle and Schmitt said that when Woody and his dad tried to find the area where the crash had happened, that they were stopped by military staff and were told to get out of the area.

Randle and Schmitt said after they had received orders, they were sent to investigate Brazel's report. They followed the rancher to where he lived. They spent the night at his place, and Marcel looked over a large piece of metal that Brazel had brought in from out in the pasture.

Monday morning, July 7th, Marcel got to take his first steps out onto the debris field. Marcel could determine which direction it had come from, and which way it had been going.

Marcel said the debris was everywhere covering a large area. He guessed about ¾ of a mile long and about a few hundred feet in width. In the debris field, there were little bits of metal. Marcel finally took out his cigarette lighter out to see if it would burn.

Not only did they find metal, but they found weightless "I" beam like pieces that measured three-eighths inch by one-quarter inch with none of them being very long. You could not get it to bend or break.

He also described metal no thicker than tinfoil that you could not destruct no matter what you did to it.

Marcel filled his car up and thought he would stop by his house on the way back to the base to let his family see this unusual stuff. He had just never seen anything like this before!

May 1990, Jesse Marcel Jr. was hypnotized so they could find out how much he knew. He said he could remember his dad waking him up during the night, and then he went out to the car with his dad and helped him carry in a large box that was full of this debris. Once they got it in the house, they dumped it all on the kitchen floor.

Meanwhile, a young mortician by the name of Glenn Dennis was working for the Ballard Funeral Home and had received some very unusual calls one afternoon that came from the RAAF.

The bases mortuary officer needed to get his hands on some small specially sealed coffins and wanted to know how to preserve bodies that had been exposed to the weather for a few days and avoid contamination of the tissue.

Dennis said that later that evening, he drove over to the base hospital, where he noticed large pieces of wreckage that had weird engravings on some of the pieces sticking out of the back of the ambulance.

He had gone on into the hospital and was visiting with a nurse he knew when all of a sudden he was threatened and forced to leave by military police.

July 8, 1947, Walter Haut, the RAAF public info officer, had finished up a press release he had been ordered to write. It stated that wreckage from crashed dish was removed.

He then gave out copies to two radio stations and two local newspapers. But by 2:26, the story could be found on the Associated Press.

It simply stated that USAF was here today and it stated that the flying disc had been located.

Calls began coming into the base from every corner of the world. Lt. Shirkey watched as Military Police moved wreckage onto a C-54 from a Transport Unit.

So, he could see better, Shirkey moved around Col. Blanchard, who was not happy with all the calls that were coming in. Blanchard decided to leave the debris field and left instructions for everyone that he was 'on leave.'

Headquarters Gets Involved

Blanchard had sent Marcel to work at another Air field and report to the Brig.

Marcel revealed to Haut years later that he had taken some of the debris into Ramey's office so Ramey could see what they had found. The material was left lying there so when Ramey came back he could see it, it would be there for him to look at and go over.

When Ramey got back, he wanted to see the exact location where the debris had been found. So, Ramey and Marcel went down the hall to a map room. When they got back to the room, all the original wreckage was "gone," and a weather balloon had been spread out all over the floor. Major Cashon took a picture of Marcel with the weather balloon.

At this point, it was reported that Ramey realized that it was parts of a weather balloon. He was told by General Dubose that this was going to be a "cover story." The balloon part that is what would be told to the public.

Later on, that day, in the afternoon, the original press release about the UFO was rescinded, and all copies picked up from the newspaper offices and the radio stations.

The next day, July 9th, another press release went out stating that the 509th Bomb Group had mistakenly identified a weather balloon for a UFO.

Then on July 9th, when the reports went out that the crashed object was a weather balloon, there were cleanup crews out there getting rid of the evidence.

Bud Payne, another rancher at Corona, was out trying to round up a stray cow when the military saw him and he was physically carried off the ranch owned by the Fosters. Broadcasters Walt Whitmore and Judd Roberts were told to go away when they approached the debris area.

So, let me see, Government ground belongs to the government and Our land that we paid for, not land the government paid for, belongs to the government as well. Is that what it sounds like to you?

When the wreckage "FROM THE UFO" was brought in to the Area 51, it got crated and stored in a hangar.

Now, meanwhile, back in town, Lyman Strickland and Walt Whitmore ran into their buddy, Mack Brazel, that was being escorted to Roswell Paper Office by not one, not two, but THREE military officers.

Brazel totally ignored Strickland and Whitmore, which was totally unlike Brazel. When he got to the newspaper office, his story had changed.

He told the newspaper now that he found all the debris on June 14. He also told them that he had found weather devices two other times, but what he found this time was not a weather balloon.

The Associated Press story carried this: "Reports of flying saucers whizzing through the sky fell off sharply today as the Army and the Navy began a concentrated campaign to stop the rumors."

The story went on to report that the AAF Headquarters located in Washington had "given blistering rebuke to the Roswell officers."

From that time, the military has worked hard at trying to convince the news that what was found at Roswell was just a weather balloon.

Dennis met with the nurse the very next day. She let him know that bodies were found in that wrecked UFO and she drew pictures of them on a prescription pad. In a few days, that nurse was transferred to England; her whereabouts to this day remain unknown.

At the time, a farmer/rancher; Mac Brazel found some strange looking metal strewn over his farm. He picked it up and took it the authorities in Roswell. Commanding Officer, Colonel Blanchard ordered an investigation. A statement was issued to the press that said they had found some "flying disk."

After this, the Army came back and retracted what they had said earlier and said it was probably shrapnel that was from a weather balloon. It took 30 years for Roswell conspiracy theories to really get started growing from this one incident.

95% of Americans have heard or read something about UFOs. 57% believe they are real.

Former Presidents Reagan and Carter claim that they have seen a UFO. Many are convinced that the U.S. government but mainly the CIA are the ones involved in a massive cover-up and conspiracy of the whole issue.

October 20, 1960, Minneapolis, Minnesota- The CIA becomes concerned about the Soviets and UFO reports. They checked the Soviet press for any UFO sightings, but could not find any.

They felt that with the absence of reports, this could only mean one thing and that was deliberate Soviet Government involvement. They felt that the USSR's use of UFO's was for psychological warfare.

They worried that the United States warning system of the air ways might be deliberately overloaded due to UFO sightings, giving the Soviets and edge to surprise the US with a nuclear attack.

The tense Cold War situation and the capabilities of the Soviets made the CIA nervous, and they saw serious national security issues involving flying saucers.

The CIA felt that the Soviets could and might use UFO sighting reports to cause mass panic and hysteria in the United States.

The CIA also felt that the Soviets might try to use UFO sightings and overload US early air warning systems so we would not be able to determine phantom from real targets.

Marshall Chadwell, then Assistant Director of OSI, felt the problem was so important that the National Security Council needed to know about all of this so that a coordinated effort could be made.

Chadwell explained the situation to DCI Smith in December 1952. He wanted action because he was convinced that there was something going on that needed immediate action.

On December 4, 1952, the (IAC) Intelligence Advisory Committee took up the concerns about the UFOs. The idea about the UFOs was informally discussed.

The committee decided the DCI should review this. Major General John Samford, Air Force Intelligence Director, said they had his full cooperation.

At this time Chadwell notices that the British were looking into UFO phenomena. The Brits had noted during an air show recently that a Royal Air Force pilot and some Senior Military Officials had seen a "perfect flying saucer."

In 1953, the Robertson Panel was assembled. They were all nonmilitary scientists that were to study UFO issues.

They found that there was nothing there that indicated any direct threat to national security and no evidence of extraterrestrials.

After the Robertson report was given, officials put UFO issues on a back burner.

To US military and political leaders, the Soviet Union was a dangerous opponent by the mid-1950s. The Soviet's, were leading in the progression in guided missiles, and nuclear weapons and it was very alarming. During the summer of 1949, the USSR had detonated an atomic bomb.

August 1953, just nine months after the U.S. tested a hydrogen bomb, along came the Soviets and detonated one.

Concern about the danger of the Soviets going to attack the U.S. continued to grow, and UFO sightings made U.S. policymakers more uneasy.

There were more reports of UFOs over Afghanistan, and Europe prompted more concern that Soviets were way ahead in this area. CIA already knew that Canadians and British were experimenting with "flying saucers."

People had started doubting the urban legend about a flying saucer landing in the desert.

But then came a remarkable revelation by an Air Force pilot named French who told that there were two UFO crashes at Roswell and most people do not know that.

The first UFO had been shot down by a U.S. plane that had been taking off from

White Sands, N.M. It had been shot with a weapon that was electronic pulse-type and disabled all the controls of the UFO, causing it to crash.

French, in 1947, was being checked out in an altitude chamber, which was required annually for officers, was extremely specific in the way the military brought the UFO down which he was sure was here from another world.

French said when they smacked it with that electromagnetic pulse – bam- out went their electronics, and they couldn't even control the UFO.

French was someone you could believe, and he had held multiple positions in

Military Intelligence and flew hundreds of combat type missions in Southeast Asia and Korea.

There was another retired officer who did not believe French's story. And that was Army Col. John Alexander.

Alexander said that during that time all they had was a laser system and the range on it was very limited. He said that in the 1980s that they were working on the pulse-power weapons but never before then.

Except for the original newspaper headline telling that the military had apprehended a UFO just out of Roswell. The USAF then closed the books that were the end of Roswell. They claimed from then on that real identity of this object was just a surveillance balloon called "Mogul."

There remained eyewitnesses-inclusive of military folks-that were telling about working the accident and their part in the cover-up of that time in Roswell. Researchers insisted that in fact, there had been an alien ship that did crash in Roswell.

French says the second crash was close to where the other one happened. It was believed that they were in that area to try and recover survivors and parts if there were any from the first crash - The UFO survivors.

French said he had seen pictures of pieces of the UFO. It had like inscriptions written on it, and they looked almost Arabic. It seemed like a part number. The pictures were just in a folder that I had thumbed through and looked.

Ex-CIA agent Chase Brandon claimed that he had found a box at the CIA headquarters in the 90s and it was labeled "Roswell."

He said he looked inside at the contents and pictures and it confirmed his thoughts about the matter that the object that had crashed at Roswell, "was not from this planet."

So, here we have French, that seems entirely credible, and he had served 27 years in the military and was an investigator for the Air Force on UFO sightings, known as Project Blue Book.

French said he was supposed to investigate and no matter what he found he was supposed to make up something, anything, but do not tell them it was a UFO.

French said, so, if someone said they saw a UFO, he along with another agent would think up a convincing explanation for the weird aberration that they had seen.

Civilians were where most of the reports came from. We would give our investigation results and debunk it by telling them it was swamp fog or what they saw had been hanging on wires. The stories went through so many channels but found their way up the ladder to the President.

But this adds to the confusion. Why was French ordered to lie about UFO reports? It did not make any sense.

French said they never gave him an explanation. But his idea on the subject was that if they ever accepted that there were aliens coming here to Earth from outside our universe or wherever it was, it could destroy religions, along with the pure fact that our military was helpless against the aliens.

And, we wouldn't want that, would we? That would not be good for the reputation of the military. French went on to say that you are talking about the effect on the military, religious reasons, and national defense.

So, it comes down to what and who you believe?

A 30-year veteran, Antonio Huneeus, a veteran who investigated UFO sightings recently spent some time with French and is working to uncover as many facts as he can about the UFOs that he supposedly said he knew about this cover up.

Huneeus said that when they started searching all they could find out about French was that he had been a combat pilot, but it showed nothing about UFOs.

Huneeus continued by saying that his reservations about the whole thing were some of the claims that French had made, and his age, his memory is probably not what it should be. It is for sure that he is very knowledgeable about UFOs, or he could have even heard about some stories or have talked to some people.

It makes it hard to separate out what he saw and what he lived and what he has read and what he has heard.

Then there is former NASA astronaut, Edgar Mitchell that came forward. He says this is all true and real. He was there when this all went down. He was on his way to college and had just graduated from high school.

One day it was in the newspaper, "Roswell Daily Record" about a UFO that had crashed. Next day it was denied. Air Force reported it was a weather balloon.

Many years after Mitchell had been to the moon; he went out to Roswell and gave lectures. He talked to the people and met a lot of them that he had known as a kid.

He said a lot of them told him their stories of the Roswell incident. The town's undertaker's son provided coffins for the alien bodies, and the sheriff's son kept the traffic away from the crash site.

Speaking of the aliens, Mitchell says, they sure are not human. They look like the little greys. He went on to add that we have no idea what beings are out in the Universe because our planet is much likened to a grain of sand on a beach when it comes to the whole universe.

Mitchell was the sixth man to take that walk out on the moon. He was on the Apollo 14 in 1971.

Mitchell had a family friend who happened to be a major in the USAF. When Mitchell heard the stories from all these people when he had gotten back from the moon, he went to the Pentagon and told his friend about the stories. He asked his friend what his opinion was about it.

The admiral said he did not know anything about it, but he would check into it.

The admiral went out to Roswell, checked out some leads, came back and got in touch with Mitchell and told him that everything that he had heard was true.

Mitchell also said that they found both live and dead aliens on the UFO. The USAF covered up the whole thing because they were not sure if these 'visits' were friendly or hostile and did not want Russia to know anything about it.

Mitchell knew of many UFO flights that came to Earth while an astronaut at NASA and every one of them were covered up.

When Hellyer was being interviewed by Tucker Carlson, and Tucker asked him if UFOs were real. Hellyer told him, "for the last two to three years I have been looking at the evidence and assessing it much as a judge would, trying to determine who was telling the truth and who wasn't, and I finally concluded, especially after reading a book called The Day After Roswell written by Col. Philip Corso, that UFOs are in fact as real as the planes flying overhead, and there has been a monumental cover-up for more than half-century.

"This is after looking at a lot of evidence in trying to discern who was telling the truth and who wasn't, and I have concluded unequivocally that the people who claim that they have either seen UFOs or seen classified documents bout UFOs, or have seen wreckage from the crash at Roswell on or about July 4, 1947, are the ones who are really telling the truth. I am consequently, basing my considerations on that."

Tucker, in turn, asked him if it made any sense then if they were buzzing our planet, wouldn't we want to defend ourselves from then if they should turn hostile.

Hellyer replied, "Well, I think the critical question is if they are hostile? Right after the crash first occurred in Roswell, General Twining declared that there were enemy aliens. There is no evidence that I have seen that would convince me that they are in fact enemies.

What would I like to know is whether that classification of enemy aliens still exists and if it does exist, what is the evidence that the U.S. government have that it bases its conclusion on?

Ex-Air Force air-man Karl Wolf says he was a precision electronics photographic repairman and had top secret clearance for the crypto area in the USAF. He was stationed at Langley in the mid-50s. He had been loaned to the project for NASA on the lunar orbiter.

He had to go into the lab where the equipment was not working, and about thirty minutes after working, one of the techs said to him in a nervous way that they had discovered a 'base' on the moon on the back side of it. He then proceeded to lay down the pictures in front of me.

No doubt these pictures were of buildings, buildings shaped like mushrooms, buildings shaped into spheres and there were towers, and at that point, he got worried because he knew he was looking at some top-secret stuff and he had breached security. He was so scared at the moment that he did not say anything more.

Donna Hare was working for a NASA supplier and said she learned real quickly about all the cover-ups. She worked for Philco-Ford Aerospace during the time of 1967-1981.

She was a design engineer/illustrator-draftsman. She worked on the landing slides, launches slides, and even projected lunar maps for NASA.

She said they were just contractors but the majority of her time she was working in Building B. She had the chance to do extra work through downtime, between missions. She happened to walk into the photo lab, which was NASA lab across the hall.

She had the secret clearance and was free to go in there. One of the techs called her attention to a picture that had a dot on it. She asked him if that was a dot on the emulsion?

He grinned and had his hands crossed. He said round dots on the emulsion would not leave shadows on the ground below.

This specific picture was of the Earth. There were shadows of an air- craft, but she did not know what it was, she just knew it was secret, one that was to be kept secret.

She asked him what they usually do with information like this, and he said he always airbrushed them out before they were showed to the public.

Edgar Mitchell told WPTV that he didn't know where, how many, or how they are doing it, but they have been out there observing us for some time. We see their aircraft all the time. I totally believe what I am saying, and I can cite the evidence as I know it.

When asked about how many civilizations he thinks are out in the universe Mitchell says, "Billions."

Mitchell is one of twelve who have walked on the moon. He will tell you he has never seen a little alien, but he does believe the people who say they have.

In 1958, Donald Keyhole, who was a retired Marine and a UFO specialist, was going to appear on TV. He was going to talk about UFOs, and the Air Force was going to "pre-sensor" the show.

As the show was going on, and he tried to tell original statements that had not been in the "pre-censored" script, the TV station would cut out his sound. They told him later he was about to violate security standards.

John Callahan, a former Division Chief of
the Accident and Investigations Branch of
the Federal Aviation Authority in
Washington told that in 1986 that after a
Japanese 747 plane had encountered a
giant UFO over Alaska, it had been
recorded by the radar in the air and on
the ground.

The FAA started with their investigation,
Callahan held a briefing for the
President's Group and other intelligence
offices.

Right after one of the briefings, one of the
CIA agents that were there told Callahan,
"They were never there, this never
happened." He gave the rationale that

this would cause wide spread panic for the public.

So, WHY is the government working so hard with the cover-up UFO sightings? What, are they really afraid of? Is it really mass panic? That just does not smell right. I can see where it would have been in 1947, but not in today's time.

Gee whiz, we have an orbiting space station. They probably have parties with the aliens and know a lot of the little guys by their first name.

I am about to tell you about a young man who goes by the name of 'Jordan.' Jordan claims he was more or less genetically engineered by the 'Tall Greys' so he was an abductee? He was born in 1962. Now, supposedly, his mother was also abducted and the 'Tall Greys' infused her eggs with some kind of genetic coding to make him, 'Jordan.'

Jordan feels convinced that when he was six years old he was abducted by an 'alien' or 'non-human' sentiment beings. Jordan says that those that abducted him looked like the 'Grey 'Breeders' but he could not remember seeing any 'Workers' at the time.

Jordan does not feel that the Department of the Navy has anything really to do with the United States Navy.

The Greys seem to be divided into some sort of Quasi-sentient WORKERS that are asexual and on the average about four feet tall. There are some who are the dominant BREEDERS and they have very large eyes and they are about six feet tall. Both types of the Greys have on each hand, four fingers.

The government is not fair to the citizens of the United States. We can handle some grown up talk about space and some grey or white or reptilian people. For Pete's sake.

What Really Goes On At Area 51

 To say gaining access to Area 51 is limited, well, that is an understatement at best. The base and all its activities are considered highly classified. The location alone helps keep its activities "under the radar," as does being close to the Nevada Test site, where nuclear devices have and are tested.

If you happen to gain access, you will need top security clearance, an invitation from highest ranks of military or intelligence.

The government has gone to a lot of trouble making it hard to see what is going on in Area 51.

Everyone working in Area 51, whether they are civilian or military, must sign an oath agreeing that no matter what they see or hear, has to be kept secret. The buildings have no windows. Employees are not allowed to see what other employees are doing or what they are working on.

I am sorry, this may be top secret, but it all sounds like child's play to an extreme. Signing an "agreement" you will keep your mouth shut? Or what? Will they kill you? What will happen if you don't keep your mouth shut?

After all, it is out in the middle of nowhere, in Nevada's barren desert, a dusty road, unmarked that goes right up to the gate leading into Area 51. You would think it would be under more closely guarded access. But, don't worry, "they" are watching.

Beyond that gate, there are cameras focused to see every angle everywhere. Sitting on a distant hilltop will be a white truck with tinted windows watching everything going on below.

The locals say that inside the base that the know ever rabbit and turtle that crosses the barrier under the fence. Some even claim that there are sensors embedded in the soil.

What really happens inside Area 51 has led to years of mystery and speculation. There remain the alien conspiracies and the fact that aliens are housed there. One theory exists that from the 1947 Roswell crash was really a Soviet crash that had been flown there by mutated midgets and it is still inside Area 51.

And, there are those that believe man did not land on the moon, but that the U.S. government filmed the moon landing inside one of the hangars on the base.

For all the legends and myths, one thing is for sure; Area 51 is still very active and very real.

When WWII was over, the Soviet Union lowered its Iron Curtain not only around themselves but the rest of the Eastern bloc, and it created a near blackout for intelligence for the rest of our world.

The Soviets backed North Korea when they invaded South Korea in 1950. It was very clear at this point that the Kremlin would be aggressive in expanding its influence. America was worried about the USSR's intentions, technology and their ability to launch a surprise attack and coming only ten years from the Japanese attacking Pearl Harbor.

In the early 1950's, the U.S. Air Force and Navy sent low-flying aircraft on inspection missions over the USSR, at the risk of being shot down. November 1954, President Eisenhower gave approval for the secret development of high-altitude aircraft; the U-2 program. They decided to use Area 51 for the testing and training ground.

In 1980, the U.S. government said it was time to clean up Area 51 and remove the irradiated soil that was around Groom Lake. Photos taken by satellite confirm that massive amounts of dirt were removed from that area by the crews sent in to clear it out.

In the surrounding cities, there were increased rates of cancer, and many sued the government (all with different levels of success), through claims that the tests carried out there caused them to be sick.

There was a hazard involving disposal of vehicles and classified technology. Sometime in the 1980s, crews dug open, large pits and dropped toxic materials down into them.

They then burned the dumped toxins using jet fuel. Many suffered from the exposure to the fumes and the chemicals. The workers asked for safety equipment such as breathing equipment/respirators but were refused due to budget.

The employees asked if they could bring their own equipment and they were told no, it was a security risk. Several became very ill from the exposure, two died. A lawsuit was filed. It was dismissed because it would breach national security.

You wonder if living close to a place like Area 51 would make you a little weird. If you visit the little town of Rachel, Nevada your wondering might turn to certainty.

Rachel's population is 100 people. They have a very strong sense of independence and are a little eccentric.

According to Glenn Campbell, who used to live in Rachel, the town's history began March 22, 1978, at precisely 5:45 p.m. I doubt you will find many towns can narrow their town's origins down to that precise time.

Campbell tells that on that day, was the first-time power companies supplied the Valley of Sand Springs with electricity. Before then, only a few farmers and a mining company lived here.

In the 1970's, people with a pioneering spirit started coming to the area. They came because they just wanted to live a life quiet and free of any interference. Among those people was the Jones family. They were immediately famous when they had their first child, little Rachel, so everyone decided to name the town after Rachel.

The Joneses didn't live there much longer, and sadly, a few years went by, and Rachel died from a respiratory problem.

The town of Rachel has a gas station (well, it's closed right now and the next closest gas station is 60 miles away), a bar called the Little A'Le'Inn (which is a group of mobile homes organized into a kind of motel) and then there is the Rachel Senior Center Thrift Store.

The Thrift Store is a mystery itself. Clothes come from Tonopah Thrift Shop that is 100 miles away. Rachel's little store then sends unsold clothing to the thrift stores out in Las Vegas. Then the stores in Las Vegas send unsold clothes to the Tonopah Thrift Shop. Everybody thinks this cycle will keep on going until one of the stores closes.

Joe and Pat Travis manage the Little A'Le'Inn and have a business selling videos and T-shirts about aliens and government conspiracies.

Most of the folks who live in Rachel will say they don't believe there are any UFOs. They all think it is just military aircraft, flares, and UAVs.

People who live in Rachel just take everything in stride. When a sonic boom goes off in the middle of the night or there is a bright light show, so what, it has all become the norm.

Almost everyone has had to replace a window or two that got cracked by a sonic boom or picked up a piece of airplane that landed outside of Area 51 after a wreck.

It is believed now that Area 51 is no longer the perfect hiding place for alien study. It is felt that the BIG top secret military base in Dulce, New Mexico is the new location. It is the most restricted location in the US. It is #3 on the list of 20 most restricted on earth.

Recently, John Podesta, former chief of staffer for President Bill Clinton, advisor to President Bill Clinton and Campaign Manager for Hillary Clinton has added his name to a growing list of figures of the government figures that are making little comments and hinting that they know things about aliens that no one else knows.

For instance, in a CNN interview, Podesta opened his mouth and stuck his foot in it, shoe and all when he said that the time had come for the government to "release any evidence it has/had about the existence of alien forms of life in outer space."

He fell a little short of confirming that aliens do exist and that the government has evidence of such – but all it took was his carefully placed comments that strongly suggested that he was in on knowing what was going on.

When he was pushed into a corner and asked point blank if he had seen himself proof of alien life. Podesta was carefully evasive in his response when he said, that it is for the public to judge once they have seen all the evidence that the government holds.

The reporter conducting the interview sensed there was more, so he asked Podesta if he believed in aliens. The reporter was told that there are plenty of planets out there. The people of American can handle the truth.

Is Podesta credible? His credibility comes into question when you look back at some of the things he was involved with during the Clinton campaign in 2016.

In 2005, Canada's former Defense Minister, Paul Hellyer, openly accused the major world governments of deliberately holding back important information that would prove the existence of extraterrestrial beings.

When Hellyer recently spoke at the University of Calgary, he stated that the Aliens had been coming to earth for thousands of years now. He insists that the little guys have been part of developing the LED lights, his microchip, and the Kevlar vest.

There is believed to be 'now' a base even more top secret than Area 51. It is at Dulce, New Mexico.

In 1979, Paul Bennewitz, an American business man was convinced he was getting communications from aliens (yes, I said aliens) outside Albuquerque, New Mexico in a town called Dulce.

The area where he finally figured the signals were coming from was the Dulce base; a joint alien-government biogenetic lab that carries out experiments on animals and humans.

The upper level is supposedly run by the U.S. government. The lower level is reported to be run by the aliens.

Phil Schneider, a man who helped build an entrance to this top-secret area, was found in his apartment dead, by a piano wire wrapped around his neck.

Richard Sauder, Ph.D., shared in his book 'Hidden in Plain Sight' that should be told to this audience reading this book.

After Sauder had given a talk about one of his books, he was approached by a gentleman who in his prior days had been with the United States Navy, actually a uniformed member. They chatted for a bit and then he mentioned about some time on China Lake he had spent. Sauder's ears immediately perked up!

Sauder asked him if there was an underground military facility there. He said there sure was, and it was very deep and very large. Sauder then asked if he had ever been inside of it, and he affirmed that he had but not down to the deepest levels.

Sauder, not letting up asked how deep it went down into the ocean and the man replied, 'one mile.' Sauder came back with another question then. What is housed in this location? To which the man replied, "Weapons. Weapons more powerful than nuclear weapons."

Now, there are documents available if you look for them that show deep underground centers that were going to be built far below regions such as at China Lake, California and in Washington D.C. during the time of the Cold War.

It is a well-known fact that the Soviet Union and the United States developed a huge infrastructure to keep a complex of defensive and offensive weapons during the Cold War.

The infrastructure would include facilities that tested stored, manufactured and developed weapons. There was along with this a host of command and communications centers.

November 7th, 1963 the first TOP SECRET memo about the subject came out from the Secretary of Defense office. A second memo followed on that same day in regard to a proposal to build a Deep Underground

National Command Center which would be approximately 3,500 feet below Washington. This memo further explained that there would be elevator shafts under the White House and the State Department which would drop 3,500 feet, at very high speed, and also transport in a horizontal tunnel to the main facility.

Just think about it, this was in the 1960's. Can you imagine with all the new technology what it must be like today?

Close

So, in reality, this has been going on for years. Even I can remember hearing talk of "Roswell." You do not ever forget something like that. I honestly do not think that anyone of this generation would be scared if they met an ET.

I have a work acquaintance who lives in Roswell and he is certain that there were aliens in that spaceship that day and he is sure some of them did not live. He also knew the funeral home director who had to special order small hermetically sealed caskets for Area 51 right after the crash.

However, he does not think that there is any surviving in Area 51 today. He feels if they are living, they have been moved to another location.

With the way people choose to dress, and some wear their hair and the body art they exhibit in order to show their individuality and self-expression of which I have no problem with, let me add. Seeing an ET would look "normal" anymore.

Do I think there are aliens or there were aliens that day in Roswell? I do. I can say, that I have no doubt that they found aliens in all that wreckage. Were there survivors? I have a good feeling there were.

Whether they are still alive I must wonder. I am not sure our way of life agrees with their

survival. I am not sure what their longevity
is either.

Do I think there is life on other planets?
Absolutely! Of that I am almost certain.
Why wouldn't there be? God did not have
to stop here, at Earth central with his
creations.

We may never know the truth, the whole
truth and nothing but the truth about Area
51, but I, for one, am fine with what I do
know.

At one point I was curious, but not anymore.
It's just not as important as it used to be.
Area 51 I am afraid has moved on to brighter
and greener or maybe wetter pastures.

Do I think we will ever encounter aliens in our lifetime? Very possibly, I sure hope so. I have a lot of questions I would like to ask.

Don't you?

Printed in Great Britain
by Amazon